Net That Job!

Net That Job!

Using the World Wide Web to develop your career and find work

Second Edition

Irene Krechowiecka

KOGAN PAGE

To Elizabeth and Jason for doing what I should have and to Angelika whose future is bright.

First published in 1998
Second edition 2000

Kogan Page Limited
120 Pentonville Road
London N1 9JN

British Library Cataloguing in Publication Data

A CIP record for this book is available from the British Library.

ISBN 0 7494 3314 0

Typeset by JS Typesetting, Wellingborough, Northamptonshire
Printed and bound by Creative Print and Design (Wales) Ebbw Vale

CONTENTS

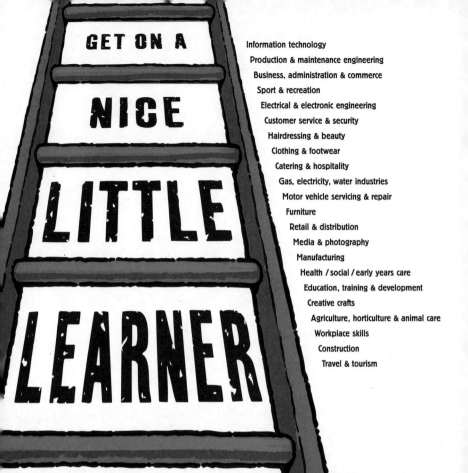

PREFACE

Every care has been taken to check the currency and accuracy of information, but inevitably things will change. The material contained in this book is set out in good faith for general guidance and no liability can be accepted for loss or expense incurred as a result of relying in particular circumstances on statements made in the book. Laws and regulations are complicated and subject to change and readers should check the current position with the relevant authorities before making personal arrangements. Suggestions for alterations and additions are welcome and can be sent to:

`irene@brightfuture.freeserve.co.uk`

A comprehensive list of Web sites, which shows a cross-section of good quality careers information, is given in Appendix 2. Updates for this will appear on the Kogan Page Web site:

`www.kogan-page.co.uk`

INTRODUCTION

> Knowledge is of two kinds. We know a subject ourselves or we know where we can find information upon it.
>
> Samuel Johnson

When I was working on the first edition of *Net That Job!* back in 1997, I felt we were just starting to see the potential of the Internet for jobseekers. Three years later things have moved on considerably. Use of the Internet is cheaper, more commonplace and has had a significant effect on all aspects of our lives. Despite that I still feel we're just seeing the tip of the iceberg, but that iceberg is much larger than I had previously thought.

My aims for the book remain unchanged – to help you find a job using the Internet. As this incredible resource grows it becomes more important to find effective ways of getting the maximum benefit from it for minimum effort and expense. It's a guide for those who, like me, aren't computer experts and don't have unlimited time and money to spend on exploring the Internet.

There are times when I wonder about the wisdom of writing a book as a guide to such a fast changing medium. But my rationale is that a book is accessible to those who wouldn't have the confidence or time to go and seek out all this information on-line. Internet users need techniques to help them benefit from this rich resource. Technicalities change, addresses change, sites come and go. Because this book concentrates on techniques rather than technicalities, what you learn here is adaptable to change.

Effective job search requires access to accurate, relevant and up-to-date information. Computers are unsurpassable in their ability to store, update and process data, so are an excellent tool for researching careers and finding vacancies. Organizations that create and collect such information want it to reach as many people as possible. The Internet enables them to do this on a huge scale. You can select from some of the best information, advice and help available and find thousands of current vacancies anywhere in the world. If you know where to look, it will be less time consuming and more productive than any other method. *Net that Job* identifies the best sources of information. It explains and examines the contribution Web-based resources can make to career planning and job search, listing and describing sites relevant to each stage of the process.

The unlimited information available on the Internet can bring problems sooner than solutions. Some is excellent, some mediocre, some positively harmful. This book will help you evaluate the quality of information and discriminate between the worthwhile and the worthless.

The advice given and techniques described applied before the Internet existed and will continue to apply in the future. They concentrate on human communication and interaction, which makes use of all the tools available. Using the Internet as part of your career planning and job search is a way of demonstrating you have the abilities, qualities and attitudes employers are looking for. It provides evidence of your ability to use the communication technology of the future.

1

THE WEB

Looking for a job is time consuming. It doesn't matter whether it's your first or your tenth, the whole process of finding vacancies that suit you, writing the sort of application that gets an interview, then being able to deliver a stunning performance under pressure is not an easy task. But like anything else that seems daunting at the outset, knowing exactly what to expect and being prepared reduces it to manageable proportions.

The internet makes it easy to do all this. Recruitment sites are one of the fastest growing areas on the Web. They offer something for everyone and, if you know where to look, can take much of the hard work out of job hunting. Once you've found jobs to apply for, the internet has all the information needed to help you make the sort of application that gets you to the next stage. To turn up at an interview without having used the Web to research the occupational sector and specific employer is to put yourself at grave disadvantage.

A CHANGING WORLD

The world of work changes to reflect a changing world. Predictions about how things will alter in the future are nearly always wrong. It's more useful to look at what is happening now, and the implications this has for jobseekers.

- Unskilled jobs are decreasing, but jobs at all levels increasingly require computer literacy.
- Employers look for evidence of adaptability to change and willingness to use new technologies.

- People are more likely to change jobs, even career areas, several times in their working life.
- Globalization of the labour market is a reality; you may be competing for work against someone on the other side of the world.
- Technological developments mean a wider range of work can be done from home or locations other than the conventional workplace. This removes geographical restrictions, and increases the need for computer competency.

The continuing development of information and communication technologies is changing the way we work. It's essential for jobseekers to acquire skills that show they are comfortable with these technologies and able to adapt to the changes they bring.

DISPELLING SOME MYTHS

The growth and use of the internet generate much discussion. Although telephones and computers have a significant effect on our daily lives, we hardly notice them and they no longer arouse much interest or controversy. By combining these two technologies, the internet has created a new culture with its own language and conventions, and has led to new worries about how it affects our lives. Some of the adverse publicity it receives serves to put many off finding out more. A network of computers simply transmits the ideas of others. The use to which it is put depends on participating individuals.

For those who have read or heard about the internet rather than used it, it's easy to find reasons for not becoming involved:

'I don't like computers or the people who appear obsessed with them.'

Have you given computers a chance? Don't write off the possibility of a satisfying, productive and non-obsessive relationship with one until you do. Let a friend show you, or join a class. There are increasing numbers of Information Technology training opportunities, many of them free. For details see page 164. Most jobs, regardless of level or occupational sector, require some familiarity with Information Technology. Lack of it, or reluctance to acquire it, is increasingly likely to prevent you from getting a job. Most UK companies are connected to the internet and they increasingly expect all staff to have an understanding of it.

'Careers guidance is a personal thing, how can a computer have anything to offer me?'

Guidance needs to be supported by accurate information. Computerized packages that can store and process information related to career choice are widely used and seen as a valuable aid. The internet provides you with links to some of the best guidance resources and to people who can help you benefit from them. However, using the Web should only form a part of the careers guidance and job seeking process. It should enhance, not replace, other means of communication and research.

'I can't afford to buy a computer and all the other expensive hardware and software needed for an internet connection.'

Computers have come down in price. A basic machine that's internet-ready costs less than £400 – but you don't need to have your own computer. Details of TV, mobile phone and public internet access are explained in Appendix 1.

'There's so much jargon associated with it, I don't think I could ever understand it.'

Anything new needs new words to describe it. Words and phrases that are associated with internet use are explained simply in the glossary at the end of the book.

'It's an ever-changing medium, anything you learn is out of date before you can put it to use.'

It does change quickly, that's one of its advantages over other media. At its best this means information is regularly updated. The structure of the Web enables providers to communicate details of changes easily. Anything you learn about using the Web effectively will help you make use of developments and improvements. Once you understand the basic techniques you'll be able to apply them to updated software.

'I've heard that people can become addicted to the internet.'

True. The aim of this book is to help you use the enormous potential it has without becoming addicted, distracted or bankrupt!

'All the information on the Web is somewhere else too so why bother?'

That's not necessarily the case. Some material is only available on the Web. Even when there is a paper version, the Web is one of the easiest ways to find and access information. It's always open and available. For job vacancies it is often more up to date than paper publications. You can see a post advertised, get a detailed job description, company information and application form before the vacancy appears in print. The way information is presented on the Web enables you to make links you may not have otherwise thought of, which gives greater depth and breadth to your research.

'People say it takes ages to get anywhere and that WWW stands for World Wide Wait.'

It can take a long time to access some pages whilst others appear almost instantaneously. The time taken to transfer information depends on a number of factors that are explained in Appendix 1, where you will also find techniques and suggestions for optimizing the speed at which you receive information.

'It's a good way of infecting your computer with viruses.'

True, and they can do a lot of harm. It's essential to install and maintain an up-to-date virus check program. Further details about this can be found in Appendix 1 on page 138.

'There's too much information, it takes too long to find anything worthwhile.'

True, if you let it. This book aims to help you avoid that. Like any web, it is a beguiling, attractive creation that it's all too easy to get trapped in. You need to work out what you want and then conduct focused searches. All the techniques are in the following chapters.

'A lot of the information is of poor quality . . . it's too unregulated to be of real use.'

The internet is unregulated. It works like a cooperative rather than a corporation. That doesn't necessarily mean the material is poor. You need to be discriminating and assess what you're looking at.

'Some of the best sites are protected by passwords and you need to subscribe before you can access them.'

All the sites referred to in this book have free access. Some ask you to register and issue a password but there is no cost involved. They do it to make sure only **you** can access any personal information.

'It's too distracting, you'll spend time looking at interesting links and never get round to finding a job . . .'

. . . or writing a book! The Web's potential for distraction is the biggest problem and the biggest attraction. Having been thoroughly distracted I've managed to devise search and browsing techniques that help minimize temptation. However, sometimes even distractions can prove useful.

'All the jobs advertised on the internet are for graduates in Information Technology, and they're mainly in the USA.'

That was the case a few years ago. It's now possible to find jobs in all occupational sectors, at all levels, in most countries. Use of the internet for recruitment in the UK has grown enormously. It's easy to find vacancies for gardeners and geologists, cleaners and chief executives, sports reporters and spies!

'It's got information on it that I wouldn't want my children to see.'

There's a range of filtering software available that enables you to regulate internet use. Further details are in the Appendix on page 136.

'I'm worried about being inundated with junk mail.'

People can only mail you if they know your address; you can choose who you give that to.

'It sounds good value, but the cost of phone calls and other fees could really add up.'

The cost of using the internet keeps dropping. Most UK users access it through free internet Service Providers (ISP). Many companies offer deals that keep call costs down or eliminate them altogether. See page 133 for detailed information. Being aware of potential costs including the value of your own time is important and one of the best ways to minimize them is to be effective in the way you use the Web – something you will learn from this book.

'Nobody gives anything away for free; what's the catch, what's in it for them?'

Different things for different people and organizations. Everybody gains, but not necessarily financially. Employers and employment agencies use the Web to advertise their products and services, to make people aware of their culture and values and to reach a wider population of potential employees. Academic and professional institutions use it to spread knowledge and good practice. Every organization and individual who makes information available on the Web has a reason for doing so. It's worth thinking about their aims when evaluating the usefulness of a site. I would, for example, feel uneasy about doing a personality test supplied by a religious cult, but not about one offered by an academic institution. Look at sites critically; work out their purpose before devoting time to exploring them.

'It's all a bit too fast. Letters take time to get there, and give me a breathing space to reflect on what I've done, rather than having to react immediately.'

Speed has its advantages, particularly if you are an employer wanting to fill a post quickly. Your reflection should have been done at an earlier stage. Before applying for a job, you should spend time preparing for the consequences of that application. Thorough self-assessment is essential for effective job search. How to use the Web for this is covered in Chapter 2.

'It makes me uneasy to think that anyone could access personal information about me. It doesn't seem very secure.'

There are problems about the security of personal and financial information on the Web. Systems have improved, but information transmitted electronically can in theory be read by anyone unless it is encrypted. It's like sending a postcard rather than a sealed letter. If this worries you, don't send personal information from insecure sites. Details of how to check whether a site is secure are on page 137.

'I'm convinced! I'll never lick a stamp, make a phone call or visit a library or careers office again.'

A monumental mistake. The Web is one medium, one source of information among many. You need to integrate it with other forms of communication. It is not always the best or most appropriate method. You have to exercise judgement and discrimination. Always consider alternatives and whether the internet has an advantage over more traditional means. Employers don't want people who can only communicate or conduct research electronically. They want those who can relate to others in a variety of situations. It's nice to get real letters, libraries have good books (and cheap internet access) and careers advisers are good to talk to!

2

GETTING TO KNOW YOURSELF

This chapter explains the application, uses and benefits of tests commonly used for recruitment. It shows how material freely available on the World Wide Web can aid self-assessment and prepare you for tests used by employers.

WHAT ARE YOU LIKE?

Think about it this way – if you are no good at maths you won't enjoy being a mathematician. Sounds simple, doesn't it? But you'd be surprised how many people are working in jobs they simply hate because they didn't go in for a bit of self-analysis before taking them on.

GTI Web site `www.gti.co.uk`

Work makes up a large part of our lives. Being unhappy at work is destructive; finding something that matches your personality and skills is motivating. To find out what that is, you need a clear idea of:

- what you're good at;
- what you like and dislike;
- what sort of lifestyle you want;
- what you expect from, and want to give to, your employer.

Different personalities are suited to different types of work. To plan a career you need to think about what you're like and match jobs to those characteristics. Looking at your personality, aptitudes and abilities will give you the information you need to identify career areas that are realistic and worth investing time and effort in. If you're confident about your suitability for a particular career, it will be much easier to communicate that to a potential employer.

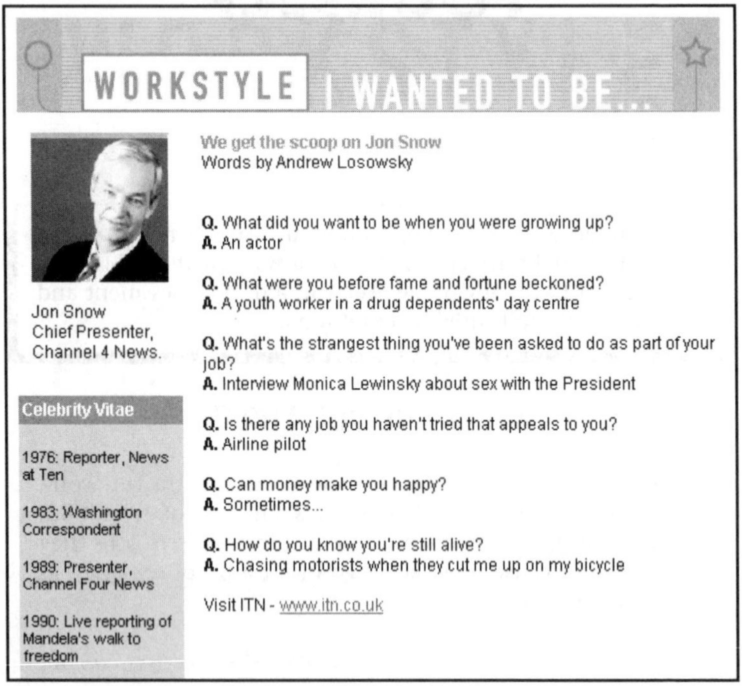

Figure 2.1 Discover the career dreams of celebrities from the Workstyle section of `www.revolver.com`

> If you don't know what your good points are, it will be difficult to convince an employer that you have any.

Looking objectively at yourself and describing what you find gives you the raw material for application forms and interviews. You have to be able to articulate your strengths, abilities and qualities; it's something you will be asked to do repeatedly when applying for jobs.

Applying for jobs means subjecting yourself to scrutiny by others who will measure you against their predetermined standards. Assessing yourself first and seeing what they are likely to find can give you the confidence to tackle this potentially stressful situation and stop you targeting jobs that you have no chance of getting.

Employers aren't secretive about their selection criteria. It's in everyone's interest that unsuitable applications should be avoided. They are looking for evidence that you have considered the requirements of the post and found they match your capabilities and aspirations. Many use their Web sites to help applicants see how well they could meet the needs of the company and discourage unsuitable candidates at an early stage.

Looking at yourself objectively, deciding on priorities and seeing yourself as others do is not easy. Most people feel comfortable undertaking a light-hearted quiz in a magazine that claims to shed light on their personality, but less so when undertaking a more scientifically devised test – particularly if the results contribute towards a decision on their suitability for a job or promotion. Tests of various types are widely used as part of selection by employers. Doing some yourself is a way of starting to measure your skills, aptitudes and preferences in a detached and methodical manner, and a good preparation for the real thing.

> You can't change your characteristics and abilities, but if you know what to expect from a test you'll be more relaxed and more likely to do justice to yourself.

USING THE WEB FOR SELF-ASSESSMENT

There are hundreds of sites offering personality, aptitude, vocational interest and intelligence tests. These range from fun exercises to serious assessment instruments. All have a value because anything that makes you stop and think about yourself in a systematic way is useful. If you're going to make use of freely available IQ, aptitude and personality tests, a basic understanding of their function, potential benefits and limitations will help you choose the most appropriate ones and distinguish between the useful and the useless.

SELF-ASSESSMENT TOOLS

Interest inventories

Interest inventories are a good starting point for thinking about your career development. They make you look at your interests and preferences and relate these to occupational areas or specific jobs. Interest inventories form a useful basis for discussion and can help broaden ideas and options, or serve to confirm the suitability of existing ideas. They are not tests. They do not have right or wrong answers and they do not claim to predict success. They are looking at likes and dislikes, not abilities.

In some cases an individual's skills and abilities match their preferences. People often like doing what they know they are good at – but not always. You can like music, but be hopeless at it, you can enjoy communicating with people but they may not enjoy listening to you. An interest inventory produces a snapshot of how you feel at one particular time. Likes and dislikes, interests and preferences can and do change. The results of an interest inventory should be treated as if they have a 'best before date' of no more than a year.

> Results from tests are suggestions to be explored and discussed, rather than a prescription for the future. They have to be balanced by other factors.

One of the best free interest inventories on the Web is 'Quick Match' from the Prospects Web (see Figure 2.2). The short questionnaire matches you to job areas and specific occupations from their comprehensive occupations database. Commercial interest inventories such as 'Adult Directions' are not available through the Web, but can be used for free at a local careers centre or adult guidance service. You can find details of your nearest office from the Connexions Card Web site:
`www.dfee.gov.uk/lcard`

When evaluating the potential usefulness of a Web-based interest inventory, look for:

- **Where it originates.** Those from providers of quality information like careers advisory services, schools and universities are likely to have been tried, tested and found worthwhile. Country of origin can also be significant. As the Web is a global medium you'll find inventories from different countries that may refer to jobs not widely available in the UK.

- **Information about the inventory.** How large a bank of occupations does it have to compare your answers to? When was it last updated?
- **How relevant the questions seem to your situation.**

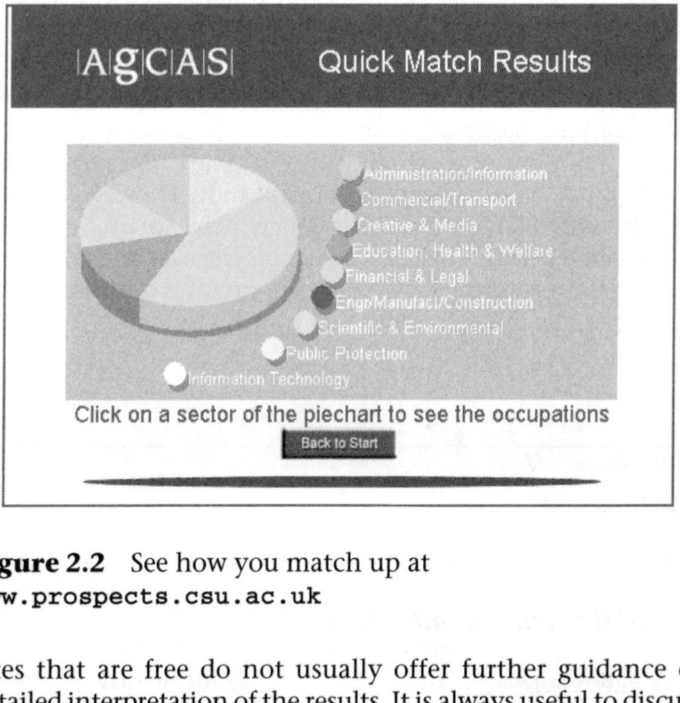

Figure 2.2 See how you match up at `www.prospects.csu.ac.uk`

Sites that are free do not usually offer further guidance or detailed interpretation of the results. It is always useful to discuss findings from interest inventories with someone trained in their interpretation. This may be available for no charge at a local college or careers centre.

Psychometric tests

An interest inventory is a good starting point, but only one small piece in the complex jigsaw that makes up the well-rounded individual employers are looking for. As well as having different likes and dislikes, individuals have different aptitudes and skills, they vary in their motivation and values and have different personalities that affect the way they relate to people and situations.

When you apply for a job, employers assume you are doing so because your interests are matched by the content of that post. Their task is to evaluate your abilities, aptitudes and personality. Psychometric testing is one commonly used tool in this process. Its use is a widespread and sometimes controversial feature of selection for a range of jobs at all levels.

Psychometric tests have been scientifically constructed and researched. They are administered and scored in a predetermined and consistent manner. The raw scores are referenced to a benchmark, usually sets of average scores for particular groups or a specific criterion of performance or aptitude. They are accompanied by a manual or supporting data which explain the theory and research behind the test and details the uses and clients for whom it is appropriate. Particularly important is the information relating to reliability, validity and norms.

.Com
Home Tests, Tests, Tests... Polls Mind-Stretching WebPsych Club Sexuality QuizCards®
Reliability and Validity Data
Anxiety Inventory
Assertiveness Inventory
Burnout Inventory
Communication Skills Inventory
Coping Skills Inventory
Emotional IQ Test
Extraversion/Introversion Inventory
Lifestyle Inventory
Locus of Control Inventory
Optimism Inventory
Sales Personality Inventory
Self-Esteem Inventory
Social Anxiety Inventory
Type A Behavior Inventory

Figure 2.3 Many of the tests on the Web are not true psychometric tests, but some do make reliability and validity data available, such as `www.queendom.com`

Reliability and validity

Reliability relates to the consistency of scores obtained in a test. Will the same person get roughly the same score each time they do the test? If not, then it's not a reliable test. Validity data show how suitable a test is for measuring whatever it's meant to measure. A tape measure is not a valid tool for measuring weight. In order to be of value in assessment, a test must be both valid and reliable. If it's not reliable it can't be valid, but being reliable does not guarantee validity. It's possible to be reliably bad.

Think of a darts player who gets darts in all over the board; he is not reliable and not valid. One who consistently hits the light above the board is reliable but not valid. One who gets a bull's eye every time is both reliable and valid. Reputable psychometric tests undergo trials and are tested for their validity and reliability. The data are made available to users to enable them to choose the most appropriate test for their situation.

Norms

Norms show how particular groups of people scored in the test. The average school leaver will not perform in the same way as the average postgraduate student and it would be wrong to compare them. For a test to be meaningful, the norm group you are measuring yourself against should be at the right level. It should also relate to a category relevant to you. If you're a college student on a care course wanting to prepare for a test to enter nurse training, there's no point in doing a test of spatial ability designed for the selection of applicants for electrical engineering apprenticeships. Some tests have different norms for males and females that reflect their different strengths and aptitudes. The size of the norm group is important. The larger the group, the more representative and reliable the test is likely to be.

Psychometric testing and job selection

The value of psychometric tests as a selection tool is often questioned. On the positive side they can provide an objective assessment of an individual's capabilities and personality.

> Tests contribute towards creating an accurate picture if used correctly and in conjunction with other methods. This can help if your qualifications do not accurately reflect your abilities.

Psychometric testing has not always been used wisely and has attracted bad publicity. However, if the company you are applying to uses tests as part of its selection procedure, you are not really in a position to question their rationale for doing so. The only sensible thing to do is prepare for them, by understanding their purpose and working through practice material. This will increase your speed and confidence, enabling you to perform to the best of your ability.

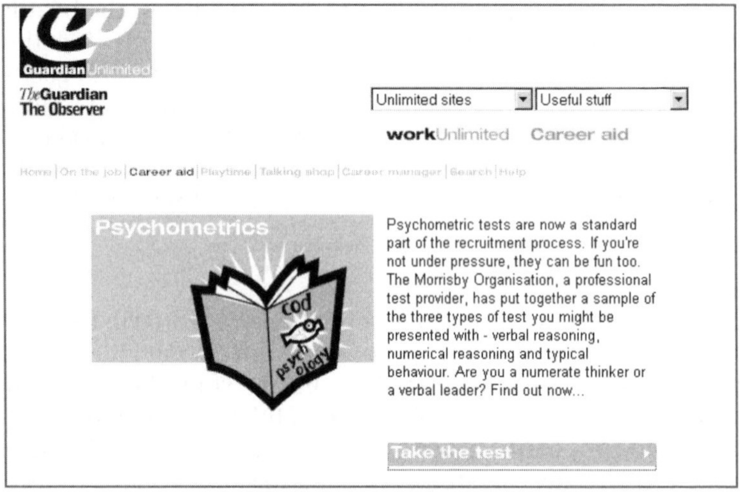

Figure 2.4 Work Unlimited offers practice tests at `www.workunlimited.co.uk`

Types of psychometric tests

Psychometric tests commonly used by employers divide into four main categories – tests of personality, general intelligence, emotional intelligence and aptitudes. Many employers use a combination of these to select employees.

Personality tests are used by employers to select individuals whose characteristics match their requirements. Abilities tested include motivation, social skills, ability to work as part of a team, determination and adaptability. Different jobs require different personality profiles. Tests used are extremely sophisticated and incorporate checks to detect inconsistencies when you try to answer questions in a way that you think will please the employer.

The value of doing such a test for yourself is that it will help you identify areas of work suited to your temperament.

IQ tests are used to determine intellectual capacity and ability to cope with further training or education. Completing such a test for yourself will show how you compare to the general population and indicate the likely level of intellectual challenge you will comfortably cope with. If, for example, you left school with no qualifications, but feel that does not accurately reflect your abilities, a high score in an IQ test could give you the confidence to return to education. Some educational institutions use such tests to help mature students decide on an appropriate level of study.

Emotional Intelligence (EI). A growing number of employers use measures of emotional intelligence as part of their selection procedure. Increasingly seen as a barometer of excellence in virtually any job, emotional intelligence is described by Daniel Goleman (1998) as 'the capacity for recognising our own feelings and those of others, for motivating ourselves, and for managing emotions well in ourselves and in our relationships'. He regards emotional competence as being twice as important as IQ plus technical skill combined. Studies claim that those with high levels of emotional intelligence are better able to manage the demands of work by using their knowledge and abilities in productive and innovative ways.

The competencies of emotional intelligence are defined as:

- **self-awareness**, the capacity to recognize and acknowledge your feelings;
- **emotional control**, the ability to manage your emotional reactions, control impulses, and bounce back;
- **self-motivation**, the ability to remain positive despite setbacks;
- **empathy**, the ability to tune into others' feelings, and understand unspoken messages;
- **handling relationships**, the ability to understand, develop and inspire others.

The good news is that, although your strengths and weaknesses are part of you, each of these five skills can be worked on and improved. It's possible to learn emotional intelligence and become more adept at handling life's tricky situations effectively.

Doing one of the freely available EI tests on the Web will show you where you are now (see Figure 2.5). Use the links they provide to help you work on any weak points.

Overall score: 66 points (population mean = 100; SD = 15; min = 30; max = 145)
Behavioral aspect: 72 points (population mean = 100; SD = 15; min = 37; max = 144)
Knowledge aspect: 61 points (population mean = 100; SD = 15; min = 37; max = 131)

The bad news is that your Emotional IQ is quite low. Practically, this means that you are not taking full advantage of your potential, whatever it might be. Low EIQ has a negative impact on all aspect on your life, from relationships (you might be viewed by others as overly a critical, inexpressive, inhibited, detached, cold, condescending, rigid, and blame-shifting person), emotional health (you might be prone to anxiety, depression, excessive guilt, aggressiveness, low self-concept, stress-related problems) to your motivation, creativity, ability to bounce back, resilience and persistence.

At least part of the reason for your poor performance on this test is that you don't have the knowledge necessary for the full development of your emotional intellect. The good news is that you can do something about it even if you are a mature grown-up. And you can start right away!

Start with identifying your problem areas. Paying attention to your interactions with other people and to your self-talk is a good launching point, as is asking your friends and partner what bothers them about your behavior. Try to really listen, without being judgmental and defensive. Read some books about emotional intelligence, communication skills, social skills, stress/anxiety/anger management, self-esteem and self-growth in general (see the recommended books below). Enlist the help of a psychologist, your life partner, parents or/and a good, honest friend. You will be amazed at how good, strong and happy you will feel.

Figure 2.5 Take a look inside yourself at `www.queendom.com`

Aptitude tests are skill specific. Those most commonly used test verbal, numerical and spatial reasoning. Employers often use these to pre-select candidates for interview. You are measured against the norm group of people successfully doing the job you are applying for (see Figure 2.6). Speed and accuracy are important in these tests; both can be enhanced by practice.

REGULATION OF TEST USE

True psychometric tests are not freely available to the general public. In order to purchase them the buyer has to undergo

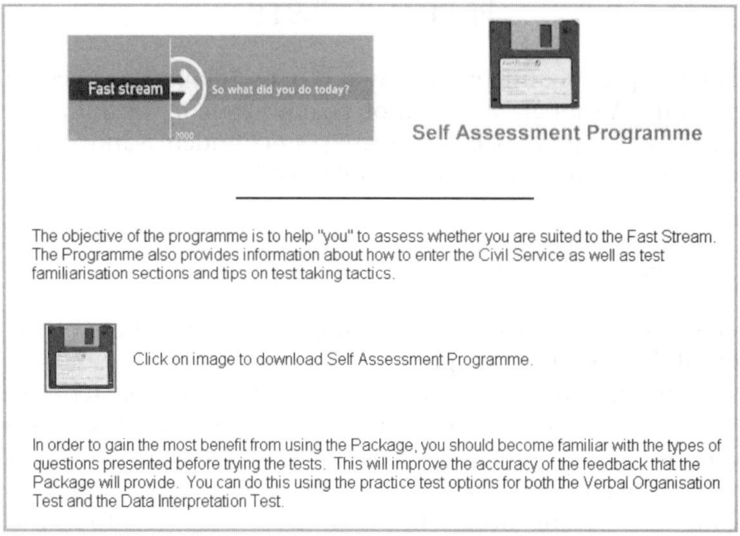

Figure 2.6 How do you compare to Fast Stream applicants?
`www.selfassess.faststream.gov.uk`

training in test administration, scoring and interpretation. They also have to undertake to keep the material in a secure place, as the value of the tests would be undermined if their content were generally available. The Web is not a secure place, nor could material freely available on it be administered in a consistent manner. Tests available on it are psychometric-type tests rather than the actual tests used by employers.

However, they have value as self-assessment tools. Many are similar to the real thing. They will help you assess your strengths and weaknesses and prepare you for taking actual tests. To their credit, most sites offering free tests give explanations of what they are, and how they can help you. Some highlight the fact that they are not 'real' tests. Obviously light-hearted ones include personality tests based on your choice of lipstick or underwear. Others such as the Cabinet Office sample or practice tests from Saville and Holdsworth or the Morrisby Organisation are similar to the real thing – tests that are well-researched and widely used.

PRACTICE TESTS

The prospect of undergoing any sort of test makes most people nervous. Although you cannot change your IQ or aptitudes significantly, practice can increase your confidence and enable you to work quickly and accurately (see Figure 2.7).

Aptitude tests are usually timed, so speed is important and can be improved by practice.

There is also a value in identifying areas of weakness. If the results of a numerical aptitude test show you have forgotten your multiplication tables, you can do something about it before sitting an employer's test. If any test gives you just a result and no commentary or interpretation it is not particularly worthwhile. The interpretation should enable you to understand what your score means, how your performance compares to others and who you're being compared to.

If you're uncertain about why an organization is offering tests for free on the Web, you'll usually find a section on their site that invites feedback and comment. E-mail them with a query about the tests they offer. You could even ask questions about validity and reliability!

If you want to try a 'real' test there is no shortage of companies and organizations offering them at a range of prices. If you choose to use one, find out which tests they are offering and information on their normal use. Ask about reliability, validity and the norm groups used for scoring and only do tests that apply to your situation. A reputable company should check this with you, as inappropriate tests can do more harm than good. The cost of such services varies enormously so shop around. Check what feedback is given and whether this is included in the price of the test.

OTHER WEB RESOURCES

News and chat groups

The Web offers access to news and chat groups where you can communicate with others who have experienced the testing

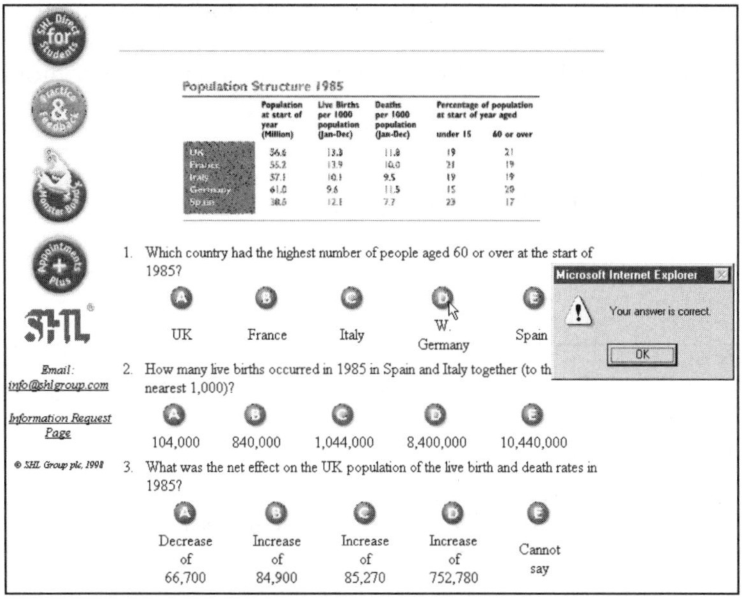

Figure 2.7 SHL tests are an excellent preparation for the real thing at `www.shldirect.com`

part of a company's recruitment procedure. Some companies like Shell International offer a chat room facility for prospective applicants to discuss recruitment queries with current employees. Other providers of careers-related news and chat groups include newspaper sites like Revolver (`www.revolver.com`), which offers the opportunity to make contacts and build alliances through their bulletin board. General guidance sites, such as Gradunet, often have discussions related to job search, tests and interview skills. See Chapters 4 and 5 for more information.

Whilst information gained in this way can be helpful, it should be treated with caution. Other people's experiences are never going to be the same as your own. There is a danger in letting anecdotal evidence affect your performance in tests or other assessments. Candidates who feel they know what they're doing as a result of second-hand experience often perform poorly. A little humility does no harm. What creates a negative impression is the attitude 'I know what they're after and I can outsmart them'. That's not to say you shouldn't prepare as thoroughly as you can. Gaining knowledge from the experience of others can be valuable if used in conjunction with more objective sources of information.

HELP FROM EMPLOYERS' WEB SITES

Many employers incorporate a quiz or series of exercises that can help you see if you're right for them.

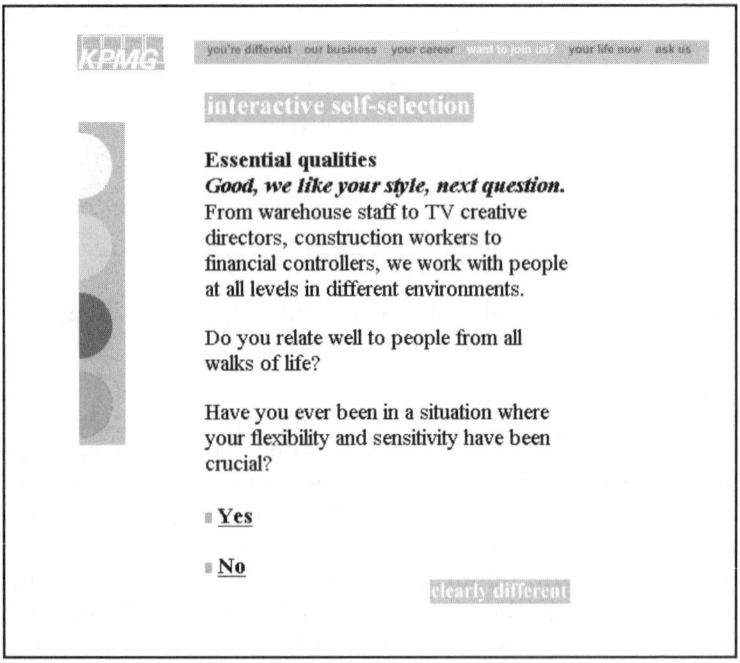

Figure 2.8 Save yourself a lot of time and effort by checking if you're what they're looking for at `www.kpmgcareers.co.uk`

Tests, psychometric or otherwise, are not the only way to assess and prepare yourself. Other information on company Web sites can give insight into their culture and provides the background information you need to complete a focused and targeted application. Your preparation will be evident at interview.

Some employers use personal profiles to show the diversity of those likely to flourish in their organization. This is particularly true of occupations that previously suffered from being stereotyped as dull. The Web sites of many large accountancy companies, for example, are worth a visit if you think that accountants just sit and look at numbers all day.

Profiles of successful and happy employees are carefully chosen to portray an image the employer wants to promote and give valuable clues to potential applicants.

An employer is looking for evidence that you will be a successful member of their team. The people they choose or invent are a range of what they consider to be ideal employees. If you can show you have similar skills, abilities, interests and attitudes, your application is more likely to be successful.

Where employers provide this sort of information, you will put yourself at a disadvantage if you have not used it. They will expect the results of thorough self-analysis and company research to be reflected in your application and be evident in the way you perform at interview. It will help you decide if the work is suitable for you, and you for it. If your certainty of that can be communicated effectively, your application will be convincing.

SITES WORTH SEEING

The sites listed here offer self-assessment exercises that prompt you to think about and build an accurate personal profile. Some can be printed and worked through at your leisure, others need to be completed online and submitted to the host for scoring. The results usually come back straight away; in some cases you need an e-mail address to receive them.

For questionnaires that take a long time to complete, familiarize yourself with the techniques of working offline (see page 147). That way you can relax and take your time rather than rushing to keep the phone bill down.

When looking at sites that offer free or priced tests, take note of their origin. Doing a test online can mean revealing some very personal details. You need to know what the organization or individual at the other end represents and what they will do with the information. If you can't find the details you need on the site, e-mail them. Most sites have a contact section or give an e-mail address.

Arcadia Group

www.principles.co.uk

The online 'Interactive Challenge' is a good example of the fun type tests many employers offer on their Web sites. There is a serious purpose behind it though; it enables you to see if their company culture would suit you.

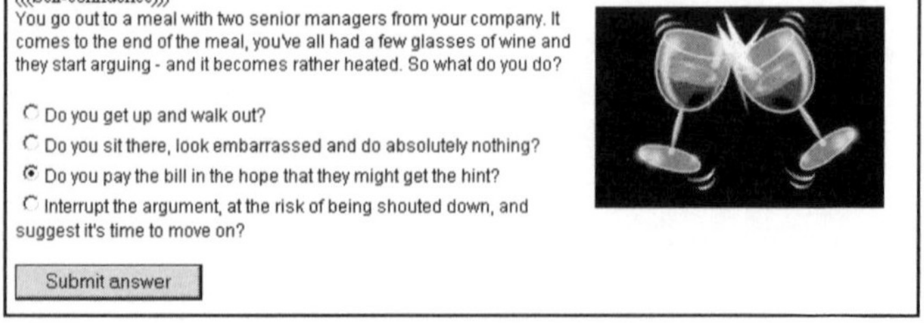

Figure 2.9 A painless way to check compatibility

Asda

www.asda.co.uk

Asda make it clear that they see themselves as the choosiest of employers. If you do their online test and don't meet their standards you get redirected to the sites of competitors such as Safeway and Sainsbury's.

Barzone

www.barzone.co.uk

Checks how well suited you are to working in the hospitality industry.

BBC Education

www.bbc.co.uk/education/workskills/wow/match.shtml

The 'Work Skills' section has excellent material on all aspects of job hunting and career development. The 'World of Work' interest inventory matches your answers against profiles of real people in real jobs and provides details of how they got there (see Figure 2.10).

Birkman Quiz

www.review.com/birkman

This short personality type quiz analyses your interests and work style that are then presented as a colour grid. The information can help you choose occupational areas, jobs and organizations suited to your strengths and preferences.

CareerStorm

www.careerstorm.com

(see Figure 2.11)

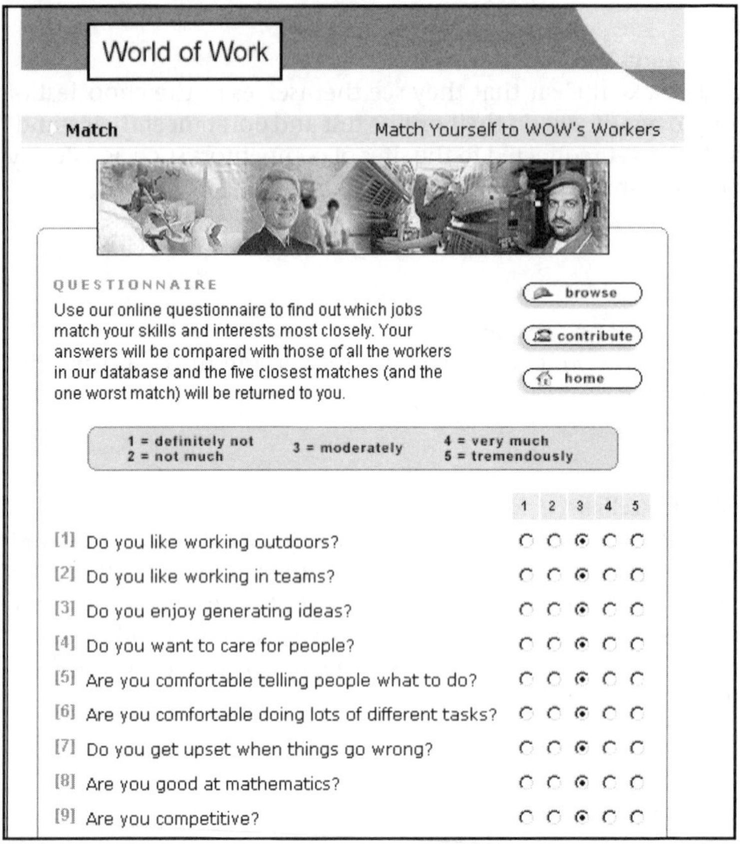

Figure 2.10 Use this online questionnaire to match yourself to featured occupations

Civil Service Fast Stream Assessment Package

www.selfassess.faststream.gov.uk

The Civil Service 'Fast Stream' recruits the brightest graduates. It's highly competitive, with around 7000 applicants annually for 170 posts. Testing is an important part of the selection procedure. Download a sample to see how you'd match up to these demanding standards. It's an effective way to prepare for any graduate level selection test (see Figure 2.6).

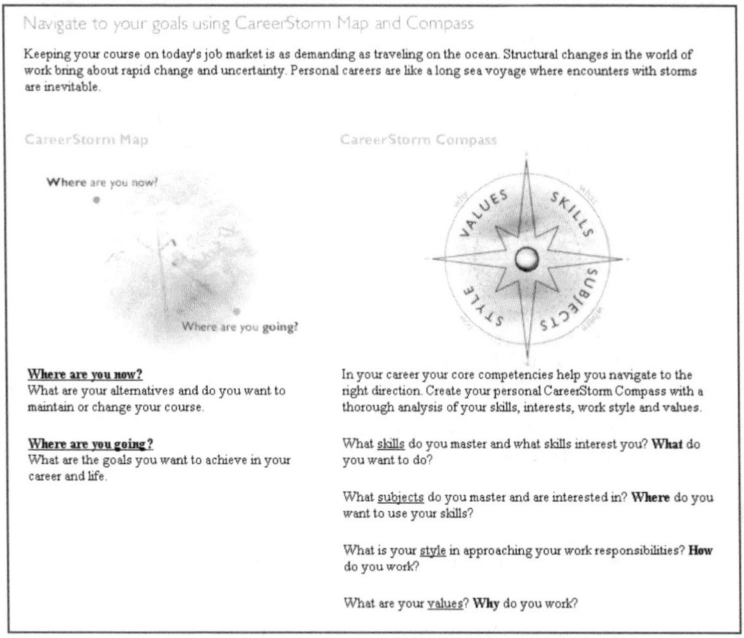

Navigate to your goals using CareerStorm Map and Compass
Keeping your course on today's job market is as demanding as traveling on the ocean. Structural changes in the world of work bring about rapid change and uncertainty. Personal careers are like a long sea voyage where encounters with storms are inevitable.
CareerStorm Map
Where are you now?
Where are you going?
CareerStorm Compass
VALUES
SKILLS
SUBJECTS
STYLE
Where are you now?
What are your alternatives and do you want to maintain or change your course.
Where are you going?
What are the goals you want to achieve in your career and life.
In your career your core competencies help you navigate to the right direction. Create your personal CareerStorm Compass with a thorough analysis of your skills, interests, work style and values.
What skills do you master and what skills interest you? What do you want to do?
What subjects do you master and are interested in? Where do you want to use your skills?
What is your style in approaching your work responsibilities? How do you work?
What are your values? Why do you work?

Figure 2.11 Detailed exercises to help you navigate the perils of choosing and developing your career

Employability

`www.nrec.org.uk/employability`

Interactive training package for disabled jobseekers with practical exercises on choosing the right career, exploring and articulating skills.

Financial Times

`www.ft.com`

The careers section of the site has excellent self-assessment tools including an online emotional intelligence test and personal values survey. The career profiles section shows the emotional competency profile for a range of jobs (see Figure 2.12).

social awareness

Awareness of others feelings, needs and concerns.

Below are the competencies that are included in the social awareness group. Each competency is defined and several progressive levels of performance are shown. The highlight indicates the target level of emotional competence needed for the specific job you have selected.

Empathy	1	2	3	4	5	6

Power of projecting one's personality.

1. Pays attention and listens.
2. Asks questions to understand another person.
3. Accurately reads people's moods, feelings, or nonverbal cues.
4. Respects, treats with courtesy, and relates well to people of diverse backgrounds.
5. Demonstrates an ability to see things from someone else's perspective.
6. Understands the underlying causes for someone's feelings, behavior, or concerns.

Oranizational Awareness	1	2	3	4

Ability to learn, work with, and understand different relationships across the organization.

1. Accurately reads key relationships and social networks in groups, organizations, or the larger world.
2. Understands the organization's values and culture (e.g., unspoken rules and expectations).
3. Understands political forces at work in the organization.
4. Understands the history and reasons for continuing organizational issues.

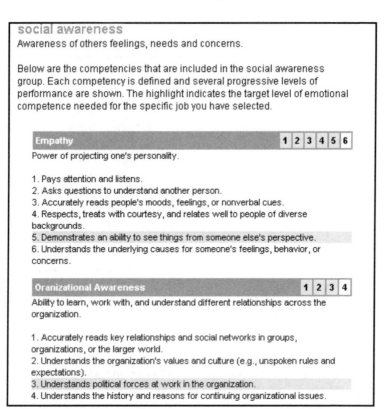

Figure 2.12 The social skills needed to succeed as a Web site engineer

INTEC

`www.intec.edu.za/career/career.htm`

South African college offering an online interest inventory/ personality test called 'CareerMatch'. Six of your most significant personality attributes are matched against similar profiles for 100 different careers.

Keirsey Temperament Sorter

`www.keirsey.com`

Developed by an American clinical psychologist, the test can be completed and scored online. There are extensive explanatory material and links to information on issues surrounding personality testing. To understand the test and your results fully you should read the supporting book, *Please Understand Me*. Extracts and details of how to obtain it are on the site.

KPMG

www.kpmgcareers.co.uk

Take a look at the 'Business Challenge and Interactive Self Selection' pages on the graduate recruitment section of this site. Essential reading if you're applying to KPMG but extremely helpful as a preparation for thinking about how you can describe your strengths and abilities to any employer (see Figure 2.13).

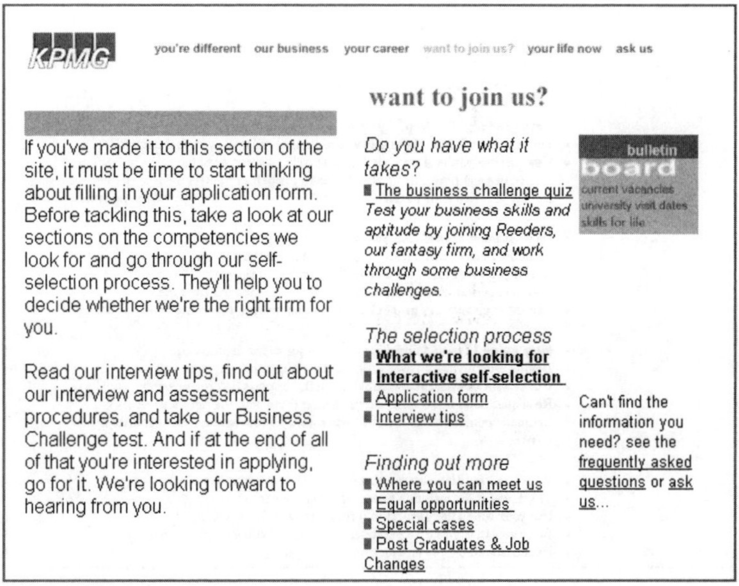

Figure 2.13 You don't have to be applying to KPMG to benefit from the information they make available

Morrisby Organisation

`www.morrisby.co.uk`

A mixture of free online example tests, including a simple Emotional Intelligence quiz, help with preparing for tests and details of their priced products.

Prospects Quick Match

`www.prospects.csu.ac.uk`

Allows you to select the most important features you want from work and compares them with the characteristics of different

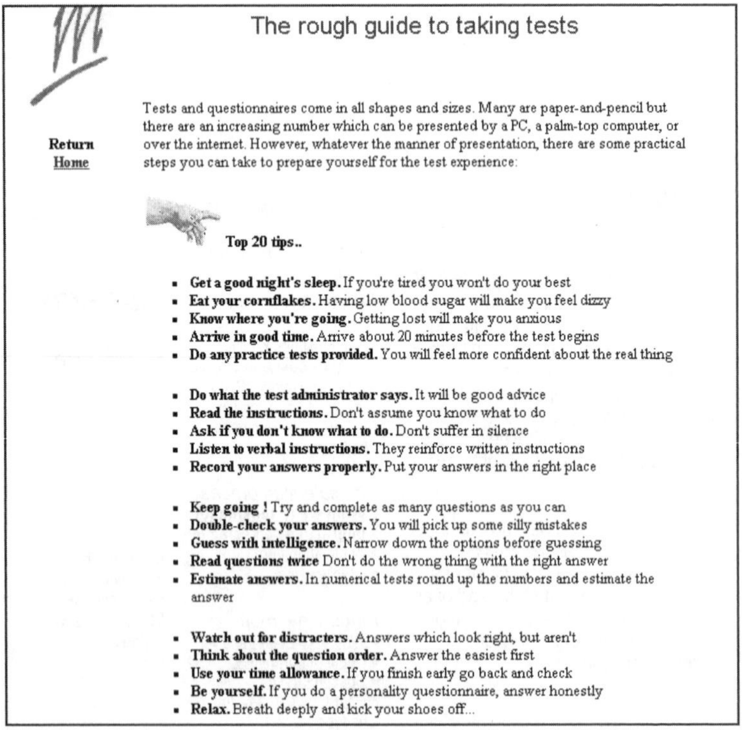

The rough guide to taking tests

Return
Home

Tests and questionnaires come in all shapes and sizes. Many are paper-and-pencil but there are an increasing number which can be presented by a PC, a palm-top computer, or over the internet. However, whatever the manner of presentation, there are some practical steps you can take to prepare yourself for the test experience:

Top 20 tips..

- **Get a good night's sleep.** If you're tired you won't do your best
- **Eat your cornflakes.** Having low blood sugar will make you feel dizzy
- **Know where you're going.** Getting lost will make you anxious
- **Arrive in good time.** Arrive about 20 minutes before the test begins
- **Do any practice tests provided.** You will feel more confident about the real thing

- **Do what the test administrator says.** It will be good advice
- **Read the instructions.** Don't assume you know what to do
- **Ask if you don't know what to do.** Don't suffer in silence
- **Listen to verbal instructions.** They reinforce written instructions
- **Record your answers properly.** Put your answers in the right place

- **Keep going !** Try and complete as many questions as you can
- **Double-check your answers.** You will pick up some silly mistakes
- **Guess with intelligence.** Narrow down the options before guessing
- **Read questions twice** Don't do the wrong thing with the right answer
- **Estimate answers.** In numerical tests round up the numbers and estimate the answer

- **Watch out for distracters.** Answers which look right, but aren't
- **Think about the question order.** Answer the easiest first
- **Use your time allowance.** If you finish early go back and check
- **Be yourself.** If you do a personality questionnaire, answer honestly
- **Relax.** Breath deeply and kick your shoes off...

Figure 2.14 The rough guide from the Morrisby Organisation smoothes your path

occupations. The resulting list of the best matches links to detailed occupational information. Access it from the 'Thinking about yourself' section of 'Career planning' (see Figure 2.2).

Queeendom

www.queendom.com

Canadian site with an extensive range of interesting and worthwhile tests that help evaluate career aptitudes, personality and emotional intelligence. One of the few providers of free online tests that include information on validity and reliability. Tests are scored online and come with some interpretation of results. There are a chat room, bulletin board and mailing lists to help answer further questions (see Figures 2.3 and 2.5).

Shell International

www.shell.com

A large multinational like Shell has such a variety of opportunities it can be hard for applicants to know which area would suit them best. Their Web site enables you to pay a well-organized virtual visit to the company. Meet people who work there, get an insight into the range of operations and the company culture. If after all that you're still undecided, narrow down your options with an online quiz to match your attributes to the operational areas within Shell (see Figure 2.15).

SHL

www.shldirect.com

Saville and Holdsworth are one of the UK's best-known publishers of test material. There is a range of sample tests and tools for self-assessment freely available on the site. There's also the opportunity to purchase products and to get professional feedback on your test scores (see Figure 2.7).

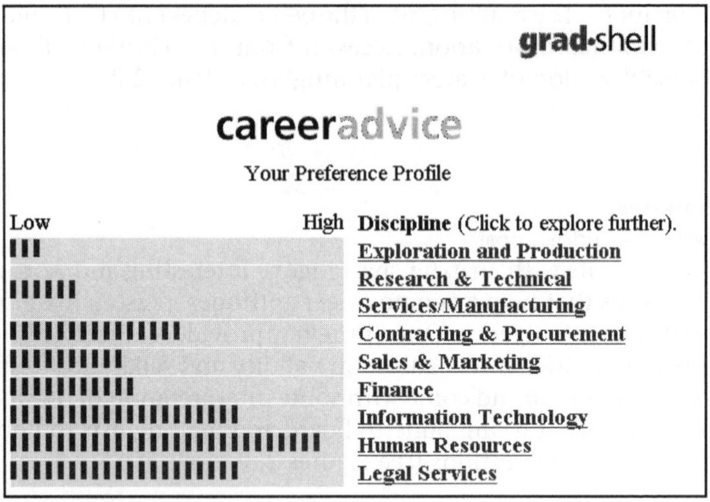

Figure 2.15 Selection made easy

Standard Life

`www.lifeoutlined.co.uk`

This site has a range of guides designed to help users 'through life's many changes'. The guide to psychometric tests has a short but effective interest inventory that suggests suitable careers.

Top Jobs

`www.topjobs.co.uk`

Employment agency that targets graduates and professionals. There is extensive help and advice on psychometric tests and the chance to complete online questionnaires to get you thinking about the things that really matter.

Two H

`www.2h.com`

Swedish site with extensive links; some to light-hearted quizzes, others to respected tests. In their words 'the tests listed here are just for your amusement . . . or frustration. Results should not be taken too literally. To get a valid result you should take a real test'.

Unilever

www.uniq.unilever.com

Problem-solving exercises, interactive games and student profiles help potential applicants assess their suitability for employment with Unilever. Useful exercises to prepare you for assessment by other companies too.

University of Waterloo, Canada

www.careerservices.uwaterloo.ca/manual-home.html

An excellent career development manual can be accessed on this site. The self-assessment section contains exercises that guide you through assessing your knowledge, skills, interests, values, personality traits and achievements.

Wide Eyes

www.wideeyes.com

Range of detailed and illuminating personality tests from the SHL Group are part of the registration process for this employment agency. Users can choose how much of this information to make available to prospective employers and gain insight into what employers are looking for and what they will find when they look at you (see Figure 5.9).

Work Unlimited

www.workunlimited.co.uk

Part of the *Guardian's* group of Web sites. This section has an interesting mix of light-hearted and serious articles as well as tests to prepare you for the real thing. There's even a test to help you see if you're too smart for your salary (see Figure 2.4).

To find further sites, use a good search tool (see page 151) with the following keywords:

- psychometric tests;
- personality tests;
- aptitude tests;
- IQ tests;
- verbal/numerical/mechanical/spatial reasoning tests;
- self-assessment;
- vocational interest inventories;
- emotional intelligence.

If you know the name of the test, search on its name.

WORTH REMEMBERING

- You need to have a clear idea of your aptitudes and abilities before you start making career decisions and planning your future.
- Effective self-assessment enables you to be focused and realistic in your choices. It will help you communicate your potential to others.
- The internet gives access to resources that will prepare you for formal assessment by employers.
- Finding out your weaknesses puts you in a good position to do something about them before submitting yourself to the scrutiny of selectors.
- Good preparation for tests can help you work more quickly, confidently and do justice to yourself.
- Before divulging personal information, check what will be done with it. Reputable sites have a privacy policy.

REFERENCES

Goleman, Daniel (1998) *Working with Emotional Intelligence*, Bantam Press, London

3

FINDING THE RIGHT CAREER

This chapter shows how to research jobs and career areas. Find the information you need to plan how to get from where you are now to where you want to be.

GETTING THE RIGHT INFORMATION

Most people will change jobs or careers several times during their working lives. Knowing where to find reliable information is essential.

Careers information dates quickly. Entry requirements for jobs change, skill shortages come and go, jobs disappear and new ones emerge. Any information about a career that's more than two years old should be treated with caution and essential facts checked. Your information should come from a range of sources, but needs to be **up to date, accurate**, **impartial** and **comprehensive**. If it's not, it can do more harm than good.

The advantage of using good quality Web-based resources is that information is more up to date and comprehensive than in any paper-based library. The same places that provide good 'real' resources provide good virtual resources too. A selection of the best of these is in the 'Sites Worth Seeing' section at the end of this chapter. Reliable sources of information on and off the Web include:

- **Careers libraries in schools, colleges, universities.** These have a range of printed, video and computer-based material, selected because it meets quality standards. Information is classified by job and occupational area so you'll find all the information on one career area together and it will signpost you to related resources. Most universities, colleges and careers centres make part of their careers pages available to any user. These offer excellent general and job specific careers advice.

- **Government departments** produce information on specific careers and provide labour market information that covers current trends and predicts future developments. Government departments and agencies have made great use of the Web in recent years. The Learning Card site, for example, provides comprehensive information on a wide range of careers (see Figure 3.1).

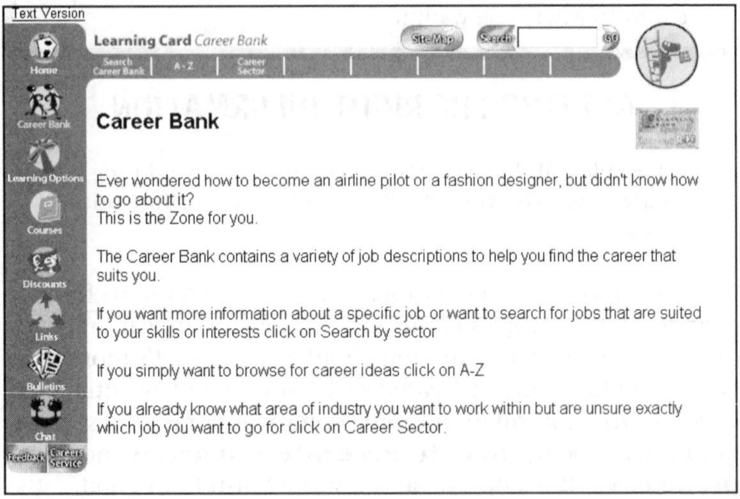

Figure 3.1 The DfEE's Connexions Card gives objective and comprehensive information at `www.dfee.gov.uk/lcard`

- **Professional and trade associations** frequently produce careers information and advice on their specialist area. Reading professional journals can give insight into ongoing concerns and new developments. Most professional and trade associations have Web sites which include detailed careers information, electronic versions of their journals, current vacancies and discussion forums.

- **Educational broadcasting.** BBC Education provides excellent careers resources now supplemented by regularly updated Web pages. Other TV company Web sites have sections devoted to careers education.
- **People doing the job you are interested in.** Talking to a number of different people doing the job you're interested in is enlightening. However, you will only be gathering information on their personal experience, which is about as far from impartial information as you can get – but a good way of finding out about negative aspects of a job. You can 'talk' to people on the Web through chat sessions, e-mail discussion groups or newsgroups (see pages 158–60). Careers information sites have case studies based on real people, employer sites often have detailed profiles of people doing a range of jobs.
- **Job adverts, job descriptions and person specifications** enable you to see what real employers are looking for right now with details of the day-to-day work, qualifications and experience needed and current rate of pay. You

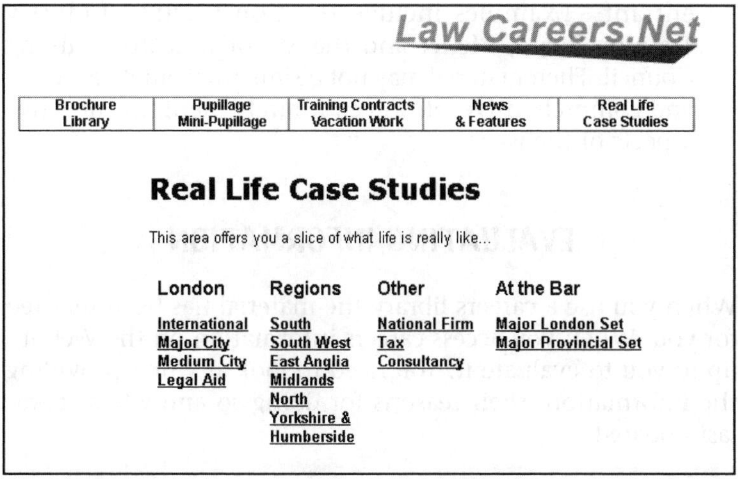

Figure 3.2 Law Careers.Net gives an insight into the world of law at `www.lawcareers.net`

can look at an advert and ask for a job description even if you've no intention of applying. Finding vacancies to look at shows whether jobs are abundant or a rarity. If you're reluctant to write to employers for information on jobs you're just researching, looking at them on the Web is anonymous.

- **Work experience, work shadowing, visits to employers.** Employers encourage those seriously considering a career in their area of work to do some or all of the above. There's nothing better than trying a job out to see if it suits you. Entry to training for teaching and physiotherapy, for example, has related work experience as a prerequisite. Many sites give contacts for work experience placements.
- **Employers and employment agencies.** Employers and agencies often produce information on particular occupations. Although it is not entirely impartial, they need to get the right person for the job, so the information has to be accurate, comprehensive and up to date. The majority of corporate Web sites have careers information sections (for example, see Figure 3.3). Employment agencies such as Top Jobs and Monster have additional careers resources on their sites. Further information is in Chapter 4.
- **National training organizations.** All occupational areas have organizations promoting the profession to new entrants. Examples include the Construction Industry Training Board, Metier and the Motor Industry Training Council. Their material may not be impartial but it's accurate and comprehensive. However, it rarely mentions negative aspects of the work.

EVALUATING INFORMATION

When you use a careers library the material has been selected for you. When you access careers information on the Web it's up to you to evaluate it. You need to look at who's providing the information, their reasons for doing so and when it was last updated.

> Any accurate description of a job or career area should have some of the bad as well as the good aspects of doing such work.

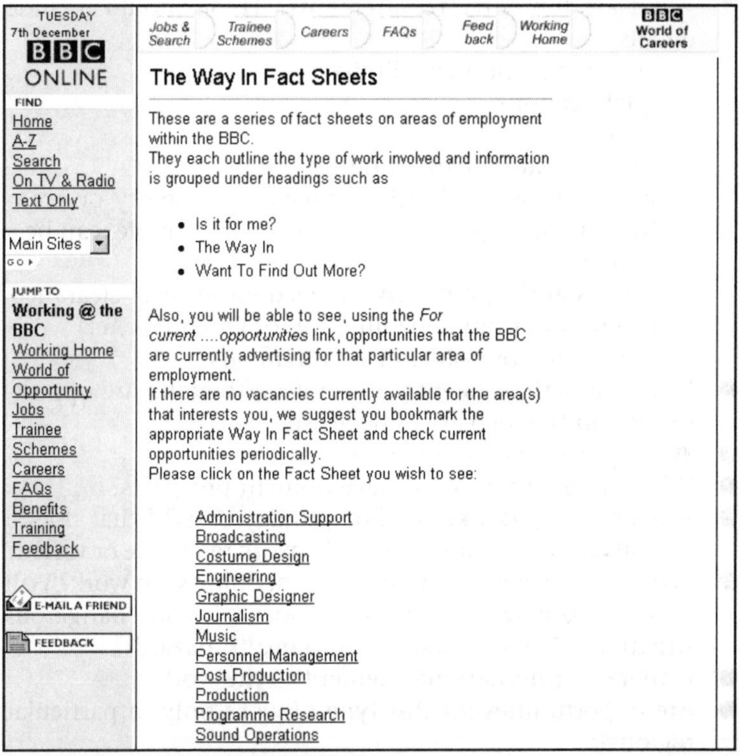

Figure 3.3 The BBC provide detailed careers information on their site at **www.bbc.co.uk**

You have to gather and evaluate information from a variety of sources to get a complete picture. Sites that provide a benchmark for quality careers information are the Learning Card, Plan-It and The Prospects Web (see the end of this chapter for details).

Is it comprehensive?

Comprehensive information will answer the following questions:

- What skills and qualities are required?

- What are the entry requirements? These should include details of:
  - age (upper and lower limits)
  - qualifications
  - experience
  - health requirements and restrictions
  - geographical implications (need for mobility or proximity to an airport or fire station, for example, can be a prerequisite)
  - other significant factors (eg need for security clearance, exemption from Rehabilitation of Offenders Act)
  - nationality or residency requirements
- How competitive is entry to training/the job? Are opportunities on the increase or decrease?
- Who are the main employers?
- What are the promotion/development prospects?
- What's the work like on a day-to-day basis? What does a typical day/week consist of? Is the work repetitive or varied?
- What are the lifestyle implications of doing such work? Will time be spent away from home? Does it involve dangerous situations? Does it expose you to health hazards?
- Is there an international element to the work?
- Are opportunities for this type of work only in particular regions?
- Where is further information available?
- Where are vacancies advertised?
- Are there opportunities for work experience, work shadowing or voluntary work?
- What are the related jobs and career areas? (see Figure 3.4)

Is it impartial?

Impartiality is harder to quantify. You have to ask yourself what is the purpose of the organization or individual presenting the information. An organization promoting careers in the health services is not likely to be impartial, whereas a site offering general information on graduate careers is. You need to look at information that is promoting a positive image of a profession that interests you, but be aware that it is not impartial.

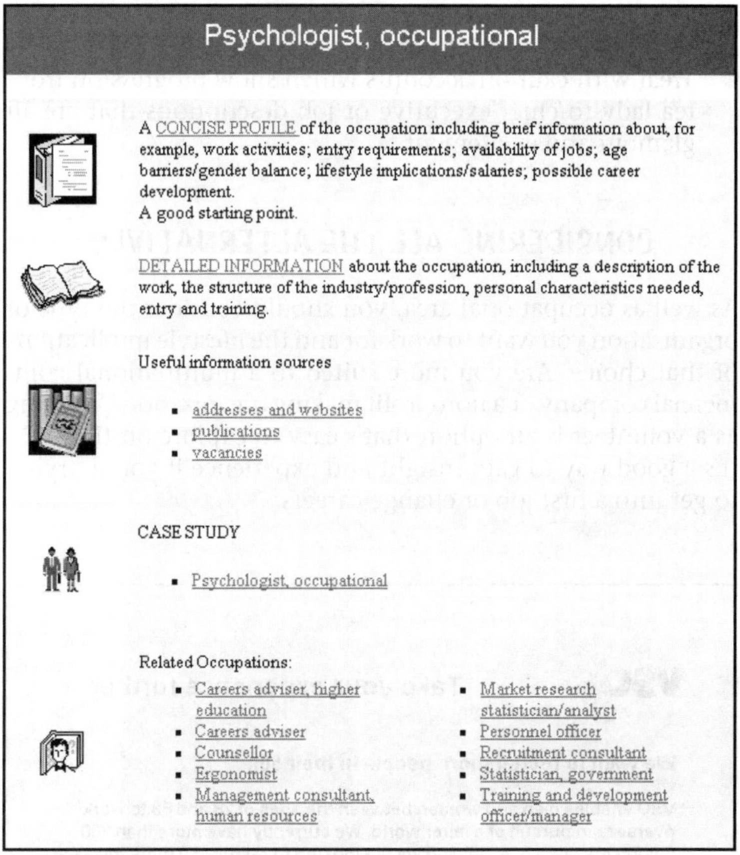

Psychologist, occupational

A CONCISE PROFILE of the occupation including brief information about, for example, work activities; entry requirements; availability of jobs; age barriers/gender balance; lifestyle implications/salaries; possible career development.
A good starting point.

DETAILED INFORMATION about the occupation, including a description of the work, the structure of the industry/profession, personal characteristics needed, entry and training.

Useful information sources

- addresses and websites
- publications
- vacancies

CASE STUDY

- Psychologist, occupational

Related Occupations:

- Careers adviser, higher education
- Careers adviser
- Counsellor
- Ergonomist
- Management consultant, human resources
- Market research statistician/analyst
- Personnel officer
- Recruitment consultant
- Statistician, government
- Training and development officer/manager

Figure 3.4 Careers information from the Prospects Web is of a consistently high standard at **`www.csu.prospects.ac.uk`**

Is it accurate?

Accuracy can be difficult to judge. Things to look out for include:

- Accuracy of addresses, phone numbers and other links.
- That qualifications mentioned include the most recent additions and changes to nationally recognized qualifications.
- If pay rates are included, when did they apply?

- That information on factors such as job prospects and skill shortages shows when the research was done.
- Treat with caution accounts which show progression from tea lady to chief executive or job descriptions that are all glamour and excitement.

CONSIDERING ALL THE ALTERNATIVES

As well as occupational area, you should consider the type of organization you want to work for and the lifestyle implications of that choice. Are you more suited to a multinational commercial company or a non-profit making organization? Working as a volunteer is an option that's easy to explore on the Web. It's a good way to gain insight and experience if you're trying to get into a first job or change careers.

VSO
Take your experience further
We want to recruit more people in their 50s
VSO enables men and women between the ages of 28 and 68 to work overseas in pursuit of a fairer world. We currently have more than 250 volunteers aged over 50, and we are looking to recruit 150 more this year with experience and relevant skills. Our volunteers work in over 60 countries in Africa, Asia, the Pacific and Eastern Europe.

Figure 3.5 Make a difference at `www.vso.org.uk`

New communication technologies are having a significant effect on how and where we work (see Figure 3.6). For many people 'work' now means the tasks they do rather than a place they go to. E-mail, access to company intranets from home and videoconferencing have made flexible working a reality for many. Sites to help you explore the potential of this are listed at the end of this chapter.

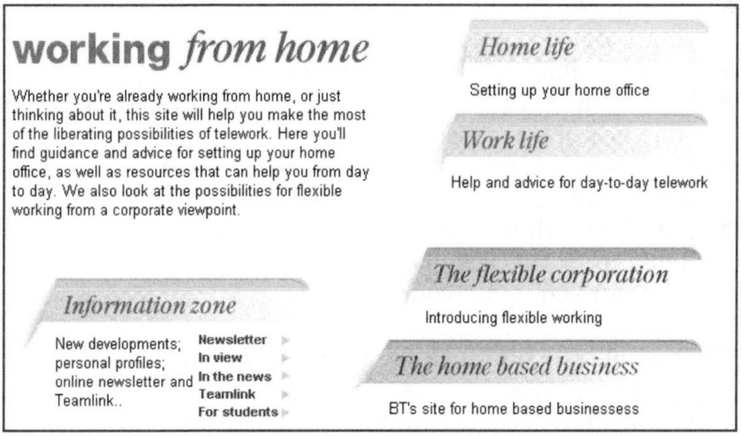

Figure 3.6 Technology can change the way you work at `www.workingfromhome.co.uk`

ACTION PLANNING

Researching entry to one or more career areas means dealing with a range of information from a variety of sources. This inevitably highlights further things to do and research and needs to be approached systematically. Making an action plan is one way to set realistic, achievable targets and keep focused.

Initially write a plan that organizes your research. Once you've gathered all the information, you'll be ready to make a career plan that outlines the steps to achieve your goals. If you have access to a careers adviser they will help you with this. Many of the sites that provide career-matching tools described in the previous chapter, such as the Learning Exchange, EmployAbility and Career Storm, can guide you through a career planning process. Alternatively, adapt the following examples to suit your circumstances.

Research plan

- Write one or two sentences that describe your current position.

- Having completed self-assessment exercises, write down your long term goals.
- List three jobs that would suit you.
- List all the employers you would like to work for, find the addresses of their Web sites.
- Find and list Web sites that offer careers information related to your interests.
- List all the things you need to know more about. Select items from the 'Evaluating Information' section of this chapter to compose your own list.

The example case study below is from a journalist on a provincial newspaper (see Figure 3.7, opposite).

Use this checklist as a starting point for visiting sites selected from the 'Sites Worth Seeing' sections at the end of each chapter. Remember to add those you find useful to your **Favorites** (see page 144). Avoid the temptation to look at just one more link, it can lead to never-ending research.

Once you have answers to the questions on your list, move on to producing a career plan. As well as keeping track of how far you've got, this exercise will help you write an application that shows you know where you're going and what you have to offer.

Career plan

- Start with a clear statement of your long-term goals.
- Include an explanation of why they represent realistic choices. This should include details of how your interests, skills, qualifications, personal characteristics and experience match the requirements of the job(s) you are targeting.
- Identify gaps in your qualifications or experience.
- Construct a timetable for filling these gaps and details of resources that will help you.
- Make a list of the most valuable sources of information you found on the Web.
- List sites that advertise vacancies or training opportunities in your chosen area.
- If you have applied for jobs or registered your CV, include details of user names and passwords.

RESEARCH PLAN
Where am I now? My job's a bit of a dead end, if I don't move soon I may lose the ability to make good applications that show what I'm capable of.
Long term goals More high-profile work. Move to larger city – but would need significantly higher salary for this. To specialize in writing about science-related issues. Teaching or training role, rather than just writing? These come out as a good match on all interest questionnaires and appeal to me.
Jobs that would suit me Science correspondent. Freelance journalist. Lecturer in journalism and communication.
I'd like to work for A national newspaper. Any TV or radio company. Any university. Myself as a freelance.
Places to look Jobs Unlimited. Revolver. Specialist media employment agencies. BBC Jobs. Other TV company and commercial radio sites. Academic jobs sites. Regional newspapers. All major newspapers – look at how they commission articles for their Web-based versions. New Scientist and other scientific magazines. Freelance Centre site. BT's working from home site.
Need to find out more about . . . Web publishing – need training on this! Part-time teaching at local college/university. Full-time teaching on journalism courses anywhere in the country. Registering with Web-based employment agencies. Web sites of major papers, scientific publications, professional bodies – look at their jobs and job links. Housing costs, can I afford to move? Draw up shortlist of places I'd like to live. Doing some freelance work whilst keeping current job. Writing book reviews for scientific magazines.

Figure 3.7 Plan the research you need to do first

- Make a list of all the things you have to do to move closer to your goal. Include a timescale for each action point.
- Review and revise your plan regularly.

The template below is one way of constructing a career plan (see Figure 3.8).

CAREER PLAN	
My long term goals	
These are realistic for me because	
Additional qualifications/ experience needed	Get more details from ....
Sites with useful information	User name and password ....
Sites with vacancies	User name and password ....
Still to do	Get finished by ....

Figure 3.8 Take action by planning methodically

SITES WORTH SEEING

The sites described here are a sample of some of the best resources on the Web. As each links to other sites, there are potentially thousands of places to visit from the URLs here.

Sites listed under 'General careers information' have information on a whole range of jobs. Sites in the 'Specific careers information' section provide more detailed information. Employer Web sites can also provide excellent careers information and are listed in Chapter 4. 'Some alternatives' lets you start to explore other possibilities that may not have occurred to you. Use general sites as your starting point, then move on to the more specific ones.

If you can't find what you're looking for, try the 'Careers Advice' section of BBC's Web Guide at:
www.bbc.co.uk/education/webguide
Its reviews of general and specific careers resources are regularly updated.

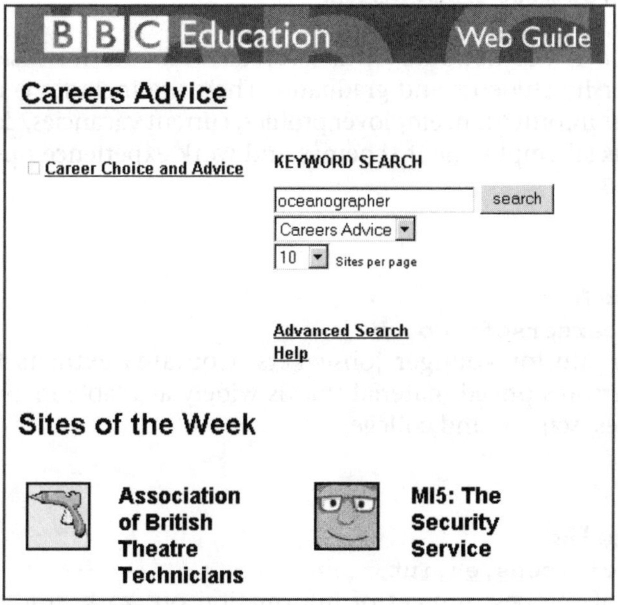

Figure 3.9 A shortcut to finding quality careers information at **www.bbc.co.uk/education/webguide**

General careers information

Many of the best careers information sites are maintained by educational institutions, government departments and careers centres. Such providers ensure the information is comprehensive, impartial and accurate.

All university Web sites have sections for their careers service. Some of the vacancy information is only available to internal users but career planning and job search information is freely available and of excellent quality. The Prospects Web links to all university careers services. Links to careers companies funded by the Department for Employment and Education (DfEE) can be found through the Learning Card site.

Jobseekers with a disability can face additional problems. Sites that provide advice and practical help for those with special needs are included in this section.

CanDo: Disability Careers Network

`www.cando.lancs.ac.uk`

CanDo is the national British careers Web site for disabled university students and graduates. Their site includes general careers information, employer profiles, current vacancies, details of special employment schemes and work experience opportunities.

Careersoft

`www.careersoft.co.uk`

Good site for younger jobseekers. Contains extracts from Careersoft's priced material that is widely available in careers centres, schools and colleges.

Citizens First

`www.citizens.eu.int`

One of the best sources of information on work, study and comparability of qualifications in Europe.

Financial Times

`www.ft.com`

Impressive careers resource including detailed job and industry profiles, self-assessment tools and help with applications and interviews.

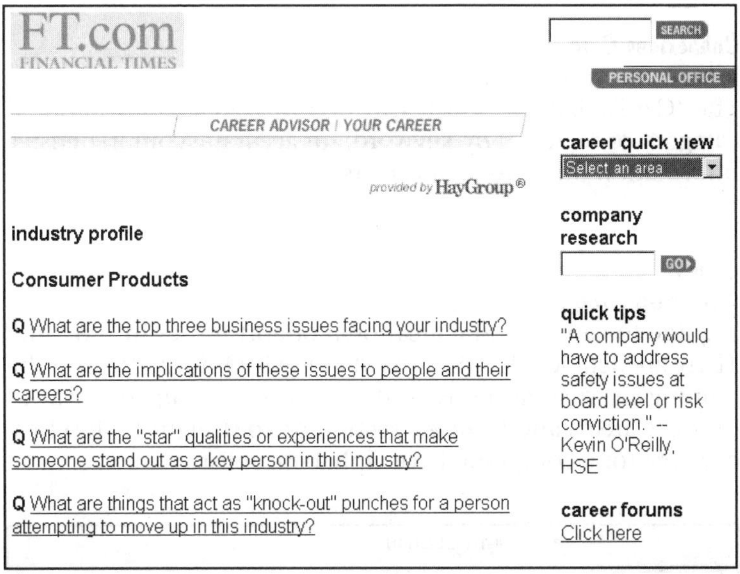

Figure 3.10 Aid to career decision making for those at a senior level in a range of industries

GTI Careerscape

`www.gti.co.uk`

The '101' vocations section includes titles such as Astronaut, Games Developer and Father Christmas as well as more traditional graduate occupations. There's practical advice on choosing careers from 'Doctor Job' and details of current graduate recruitment.

Gradunet's Virtual Careers Office

`www.gradunet.co.uk`

Careers information, supplemented by a 'Virtual Careers Fairs' – live, one-day events where graduate recruiters gather in an internet cafe and chat online to students across the UK. There's also a discussion forum that deals with graduate employment and a 'Hall of Fame' with an interesting selection of celebrity graduate profiles. See Chapter 5 for details of their reusable application form.

Connexions Card

www.dfee.gov.uk/1card

The 'Career Bank' section can be browsed by occupational category or searched by keyword, for accurate, comprehensive information on a range of careers.

Plan-It

www.ceg.org.uk

A guide to careers and educational opportunities in Scotland. There are detailed descriptions of jobs with information on the training and qualifications needed. Browse by occupational areas in the 'Careers and Courses' section or go straight to 'Job Descriptors' for a comprehensive alphabetical list.

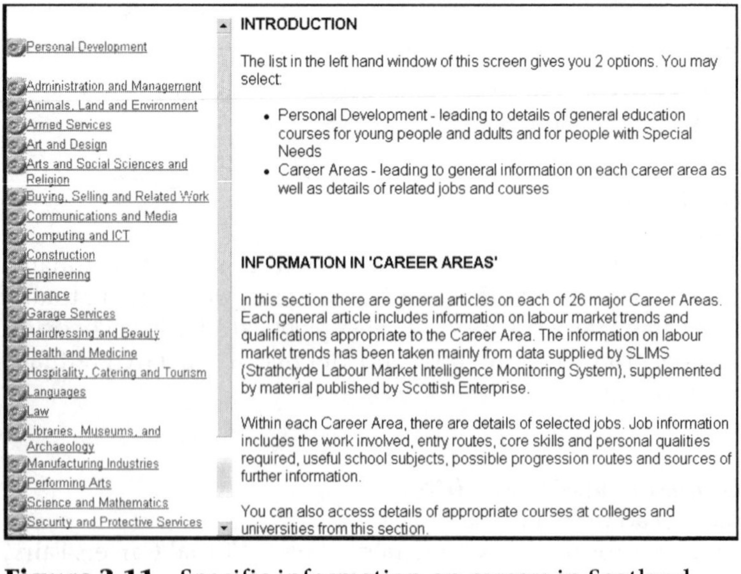

Figure 3.11 Specific information on careers in Scotland

The Prospects Web

www.prospects.csu.ac.uk

Primarily a resource for those at university, this site contains an excellent database of over 400 detailed job descriptions. The emphasis is on graduate level jobs but includes some for which a degree is not essential, such as air cabin crew, police and ambulance work. In addition to general information there is a searchable database of around 1500 graduate employers and current vacancies are advertised.

Skill

www.skill.org.uk

Promotes opportunities for young people and adults with any kind of disability in post-16 education, training and employment across the UK.

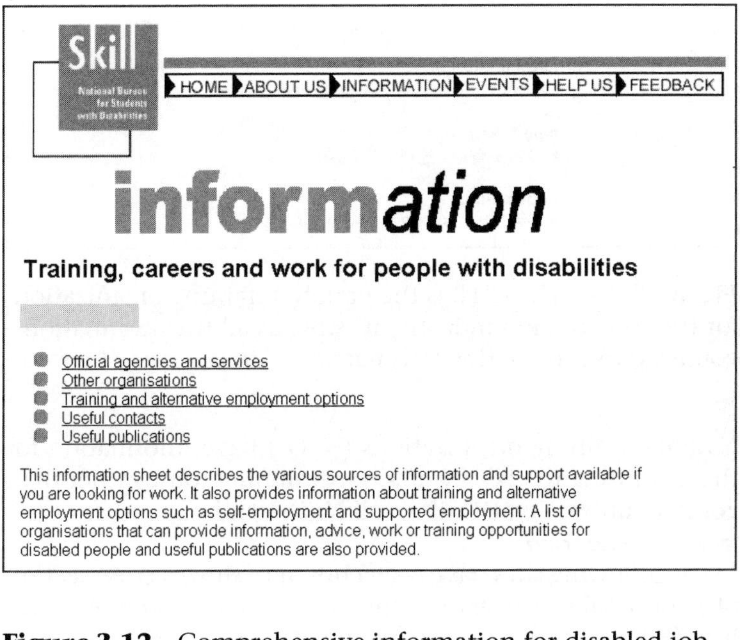

Figure 3.12 Comprehensive information for disabled job seekers

Specific careers information

Information on specific careers is most often supplied by professional and trade organizations. Links to a range of professional bodies can be found on the NISS Web site:
`www.niss.ac.uk/world/prof-bodies.html`

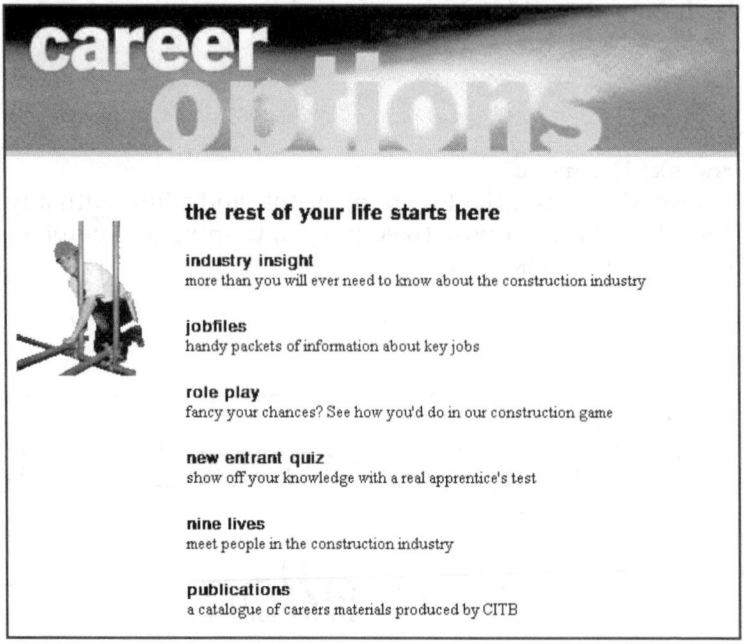

Figure 3.13 The CITB is the national training organization for the construction industry. Its site has all the information you need to explore this career area

National training organizations (NTOs) have information for those wanting to take a work-based training route rather than going to university. Details of all NTOs can be found at:
`www.nto-nc.org`

The following sites have been chosen to show a cross-section of good quality careers information. A more comprehensive list of sites is in Appendix 2 and updates for this will appear on the Kogan Page Web site **`www.kogan-page.co.uk`**

The Advertising Association
www.adassoc.org.uk

Go to the 'Information Centre' for an online version of *Getting into Advertising.* It's an invaluable guide to jobs in the industry and how to choose, prepare for and secure the career that matches your aptitudes.

Barzone
www.barzone.co.uk

All the information you need about working in pubs. Includes job openings, training information, details of employers, industry open days, careers events and a section on colleges and universities offering hospitality or licensed retailing courses.

British Artist Blacksmiths Association
www.baba.org.uk

Learn how to become a blacksmith, search for events and job openings or details of BABA members willing to offer work experience to students. Update your ideas on what blacksmiths actually do by taking a look at 'Lucid Dreaming', a gallery in iron.

British Computer Society
www.bcs.org.uk

Fact sheets on specialized computing and information systems, jobs, employers, career development opportunities and how to choose the right computing course. The 'WorkLink' section offers national work experience opportunities.

British Horse Society
www.bhs.org.uk

Training for riding instructors, stable managers, grooms and organizations offering riding holidays. The Equestrian Passport for Riding Instructors and Trainers is recognized in 28 countries.

sites worth seeing

British Institute of Architectural Technologists (BIAT)
www.biat.org.uk
Find details of accredited degrees and information on what architectural technologists do.

British Institute of Professional Photography
www.bipp.com/working.html
Working With Light covers photography careers in advertising, fashion, newspapers, industry, television, film, video and medical photography. There are sections on getting started, details of college courses and help with applications including tips on how to prepare and present a portfolio.

British National Space Centre – Space Index
www.highview.co.uk
A directory of space activities in the UK and further afield. Contains careers information, details of events and links to listing of space-related jobs. You can order a free CD ROM from the site that can be used offline with any browser and contains information on all UK space-related activities.

British Psychological Society
www.bps.org.uk/careers/careers.htm
Detailed information on careers and training in psychology.

British Medical Journal
www.bmj.com
The Career Focus section has archives of careers-related articles. Excellent for researching the implications of a career in medicine at the decision making stage, as well as a source of information to aid career development. Articles cover a wide range of topics such as working in New Zealand, job sharing, availability of flexible training for those with families, how to move into medical broadcasting and what sort of work to look for if you need regular sleep.

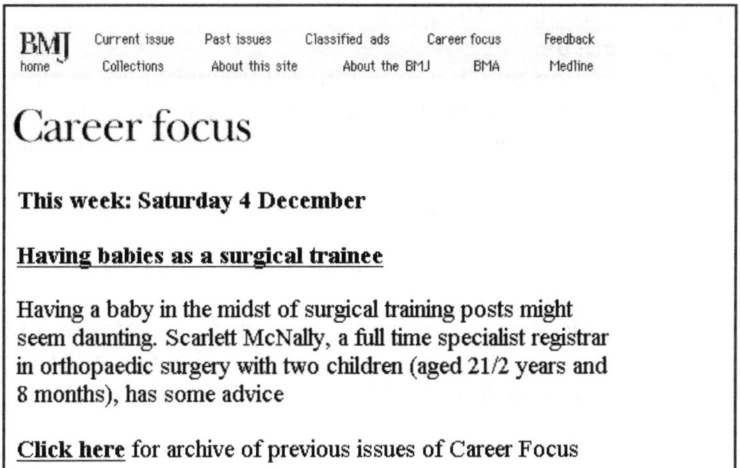

BMJ home
Current issue
Past issues
Classified ads
Career focus
Feedback
Collections
About this site
About the BMJ
BMA
Medline
Career focus
This week: Saturday 4 December
Having babies as a surgical trainee
Having a baby in the midst of surgical training posts might seem daunting. Scarlett McNally, a full time specialist registrar in orthopaedic surgery with two children (aged 21/2 years and 8 months), has some advice
Click here for archive of previous issues of Career Focus

Figure 3.14 Explore the reality of medical careers

CAPITB Trust

www.careers-in-clothing.co.uk

CAPITB is the national training organization for the British clothing industry. Use this site to learn about the opportunities in haute couture, bespoke tailoring, hat and clothes design.

British Cartographic Society

www.cartography.org.uk

The Society's booklet, *Careers in Cartography*, is regarded as the definitive source of information on the art and science of careers in mapping. An online version can be found in the publications section of this site.

Construction Industry Training Board

www.citb.org.uk

As well as giving detailed information on all construction careers and how to get into them, this site lets you have a go at tests used for apprentice selection and the chance to indulge in a bit of role-play.

College of Occupational Therapists
www.cot.co.uk
Find information on what occupational therapists do, explore specialisms within the profession, find where to study, how to work overseas or how to work in the UK if you're from another country.

Council for Education and Training in Social Work (CCETSW)
www.ccetsw.org.uk
If you're considering a career in social work all the information you need is in the 'Career Factfile' section. There are lists of courses for all regions of the UK.

Employability
www.nrec.org.uk/employability
This interactive training package for disabled jobseekers has specific information on work in the communication industries at a professional level.

Engineering Marine Training Authority
www.emta.org.uk
The Enginuity section of this site has information on careers in chemical, civil, electrical, electronic, manufacturing, marine and mechanical engineering. 'Insight' courses provide sixth form girls with a week's free training to see what engineering's all about.

Society of Chiropodists and Podiatrists
www.feetforlife.org/career.htm
Discover what you need to train and work as a podiatrist.

Institute of Leisure and Amenity Management
www.ilam.co.uk
Downloadable publications include *The Directory of UK Leisure Courses* and *Careers in Leisure*. This covers arboriculture, horticulture, arts administration, countryside management, conservation, 'wardening', parks management, coaching, sports development and tourist information work.

Institute of Public Relations

www.ipr.org.uk

Comprehensive information on careers in public relations. Look out for the annual careers day that gives the chance to meet and talk to people working in the industry.

Landscape Institute

www.L-i.org.uk and **www.1stLandscape.co.uk**

Information on what being a landscape architect or landscape technician involves with case studies, discussion forums and how to train.

Law Careers Net

www.lawcareers.net

Real life case studies, courses, training information and vacancies give an insight into the range of careers available (see Figure 3.2).

Library Association

www.la-hq.org.uk

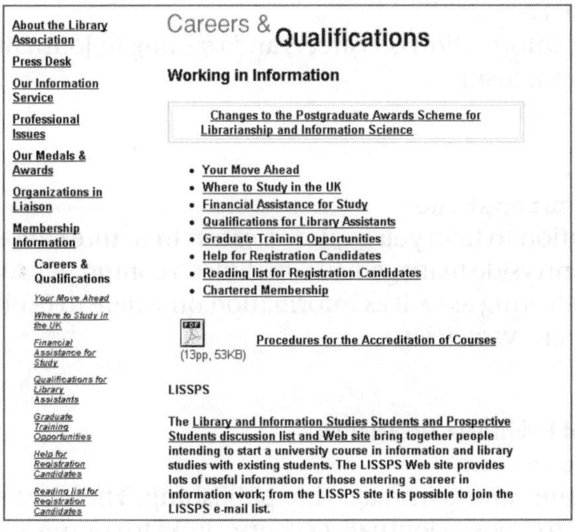

Figure 3.15 All the information you need about training for a career in library and information work

Metier

www.metier.org.uk

The national training organization for the arts and entertainment sector. Use the site to help you break into this popular area of work.

Motor Industry Training Council

www.motor-careers.co.uk

Information on education, training and careers in the retail motor industry. Covers mechanical, electrical and body repair, sales and marketing, roadside repair and customer service.

National Coaching Foundation

www.ncf.org.uk

The Education and Information Services section of this site has details on what it takes to be an effective sports coach and the qualifications needed. There's information on getting started as well as how to develop your career if you're experienced.

National Council for the Training of Journalists

www.nctj.com

Detailed information on careers and training in journalism and photojournalism.

Naturenet

www.naturenet.net

Information to help you explore a career in nature conservation and countryside management. Includes a comprehensive guide to volunteering as well as information on where to find courses and current vacancies.

Periodical Publishers Association

www.ppa.co.uk

Investigate careers in magazine publishing. There are sections on how to choose a journalism course, links to courses accredited by the Periodicals Training Council and help with arranging work experience.

RNIB

www.rnib.org.uk

The 'Gateway for Opportunities for Reaching Work' (GROW) section of the site helps people with serious sight problems make informed choices about personal development through education, training and employment.

Royal Institute of British Architects

www.architecture.com

Extensive careers section includes personal profiles, details of courses, how to fund study, information on UK and international schools of architecture.

Royal Institution of Chartered Surveyors

www.rics.org.uk

Includes the *Official Prospectus to Surveying Education* with details of higher education courses in land, property and construction as well as *Opportunities 2000*, a directory of employment and training opportunities for surveyors.

Royal Society of Chemistry

www.chemistry.rsc.org

The careers section has information and advice to help you find the right job including tips on CV writing and job-hunting strategies. Industrial and academic jobs for chemists are updated weekly (see Figure 3.16).

Royal Town Planning Institute

www.rtpi.org.uk

Career Profiles give insights into what the work is really like and details of accredited courses. Find answers to questions such as where jobs are, how to become a planner and what sort of people the career appeals to.

chemsoc careers

Welcome to chemsoc Careers - the right place to be for job advertisements and careers advice.

"**Careers - job vacancies** " gives you the latest selection of industrial and academic vacancies, plus studentships & fellowships.

Careers on the web provides links and reviews of some of the best chemistry careers information on the Web, providing access to thousands of job opportunities worldwide. Try searching all these sites simultaneously using our new careers database.

The Professional Chemist's Toolkit - a regular series of one page careers features from *Chemistry in Britain*

For help and advice on career related subjects, visit these pages:

- Planning your Job Search Strategy
- Preparing your CV
- Improving your Interview Technique
- Coping with Tests and Assessment Centres
- Careers with Chemistry - Personal Profiles

Career Management Programme and Jobseeker Service provided by the Royal Society of Chemistry

Figure 3.16 A one-stop site for careers and vacancy information for chemists

Skillset

www.skillset.org/careers.htm

Indispensable guide for exploring careers in the media. The online handbook covers the broadcast, film and video industry. It includes sections on radio and multimedia and has a chapter covering training and employment opportunities for disabled people.

Society for Underwater Technology

www.sut.org.uk

Access detailed careers and qualifications information through the 'Education & Training' link. Explore careers in diving, underwater communications, aquaculture, geology of the seabed, oceanography and marine engineering.

Training Zone

www.trainingzone.co.uk

This interactive community for training and human resource development professionals provides excellent information and resources for those working in or wishing to enter this field.

Workable

members.aol.com/workableuk

Workable campaigns to promote equal employment opportunities for disabled graduates. They organize work experience schemes covering employment in the media, law, insurance, the arts and the Civil Service. Details of all these are on their site alongside current vacancies for long-term jobs.

Some alternatives

European Telework Online

www.eto.org.uk

Describing itself as the internet portal for teleworking, telecommuting and related topics, there's information on and links to a wealth of resources, including a critical assessment of schemes that claim to pay for surfing the internet. The UK-based association for teleworkers can be found at www.tca.org.uk.

Flexibility

www.flexibility.co.uk

Flexibility is a business newsletter published by the Home Office Partnership, a company that offers strategies and solutions for new ways of working. It aims to stimulate debate about the changing world of work and present research and opinion about innovations in employment practice, organizational development, technological change and public policy.

Freelance Centre

www.freelancecentre.com

Before you decide whether freelancing is for you, take a look at this site. It's packed with practical advice that can help make going it alone an affordable reality.

Smarter Work
www.smarterwork.com
A virtual office where freelancers find and bid for work such as document production, graphic design, writing, editing, Web design and research. The company takes a 10% commission on completion of projects arranged through their site.

Working From Home
www.workingfromhome.co.uk
This site from British Telecom provides information on the benefits and problems of this new way of working. There are case studies, news items, details of how to set up a home office and practical help on day-to-day issues.

BOND: British Overseas NGOs for Development
www.bond.org.uk
If you're looking for a career that will make a difference in the developing world or some of its trouble spots, this Web site gives an insight into what's available (see Figure 4.20).

Community Service Volunteers
www.csv.org.uk
Around 100,000 people a year become involved in voluntary work with CSV. All applicants are offered a place and there's a huge range of opportunities for people of any age to make a contribution to society. Opportunities exist in Europe as well as the UK.

National Centre for Volunteering
www.volunteering.org.uk
Volunteering can be an excellent way of filling an experience gap. This site provides a comprehensive guide to all matters related to volunteering. There are links to organizations with opportunities in a variety of locations. Related information covers topics such as how being a volunteer affects welfare benefits and guidelines on what to look for in a volunteering opportunity.

Top Jobs

`www.topjobs.co.uk`

Employment agency that targets graduates and professionals. There is extensive help and advice on psychometric tests and the chance to complete online questionnaires to get you thinking about the things that really matter.

Voluntary Service Overseas

`www.vso.org.uk`

Read extracts from volunteers' reports to find out what life as a VSO volunteer is really like. Current openings for skilled and experienced volunteers are available in more than 40 developing countries.

World Service Enquiry

`www.wse.org.uk`

Provides advice about voluntary work overseas for peace, justice and development through a paper and online guide. There's also information for skilled and experienced individuals wanting to work in overseas development.

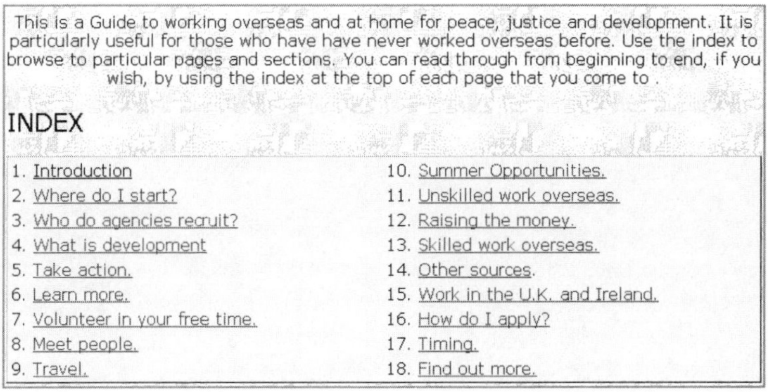

Figure 3.17 A world of different opportunities

WORTH REMEMBERING

- The internet gives access to information on most careers. Since the quality of information varies, it's up to you to check how good it is.
- For a comprehensive picture of a career area, your information should come from a variety of sources. You should be able to see the good and bad sides of a career.
- Alternatives such as working from home or doing voluntary work are worth exploring if more conventional careers don't appeal to you.
- For information to be of value it must be accurate and up to date.
- If you're looking at lots of information and making long-term plans you need to keep track of where you are. One way is to make written plans and keep reviewing them.

4

FINDING VACANCIES ON THE WEB

This chapter shows you where to find vacancies on the Web. It will enable you to harness the potential of having access to millions of job openings in a focused and manageable way. Vacancies are not just for jobseekers; they are an excellent resource for investigating careers.

JOB SEARCHING MADE EASY

Finding suitable jobs to apply for is a time consuming business. Many people stay in a job they dislike because they don't have time to look for another. There are so many vacancies on the Web that searching through them could leave you with no time to apply for work. On the other hand, if you know where to look and what to do, it can result in vacancies and employers finding you!

The sources of advertised vacancies on the Web are the same as in the real world.

The internet offers easy access to a huge range of vacancy sources. Local and national newspapers, professional journals and institutes, trade associations, recruitment agencies and employers all make use of the Web to attract and recruit the best applicants (see Figure 4.1). Each can be used in different ways or in combination, depending on your circumstances. If you want a job in a specific location, the vacancy pages of the local paper or an agency that covers the area are good starting points. National papers group their adverts by professional field rather than location, as do professional and trade journals. If you are really keen to work for a specific employer, go straight to them.

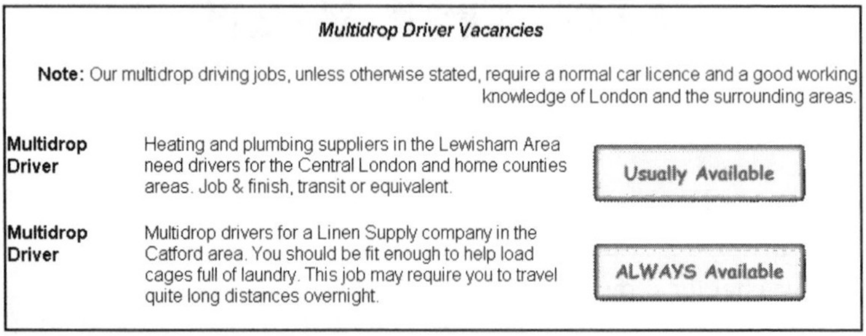

Figure 4.1 PSR proudly claim more unskilled temporary jobs than anyone else in London at `www.psr-agency.com`

Vacancies advertised on the Web are clearly for people who can use this medium. In the early days of Web recruitment the majority of posts advertised were Information Technology (IT) related, but that's no longer the case. There's every sort of job in every industry. All occupational sectors have been affected by new communication technologies and computer literacy is becoming as essential as ordinary literacy was a generation ago.

Passive search – helping jobs find you

Trying to find the right vacancies can be a full-time job in itself. Only a privileged few can sit back and feel sure that employers will come looking for them because of their known talents and capabilities. The Web makes it possible for everyone to become a passive jobseeker! Sadly this does not mean doing nothing at all and finding an offer of the perfect job amongst your e-mail, but it's getting close. It's increasingly common for sites advertising job to include the option of sending job details to you.

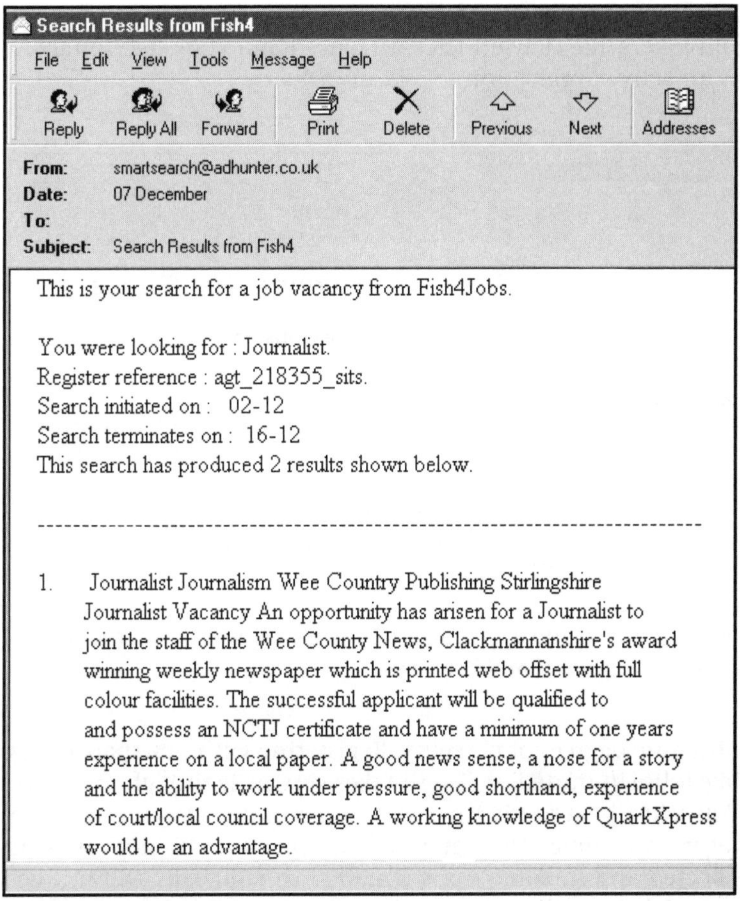

Search Results from Fish4

File Edit View Tools Message Help

Reply Reply All Forward Print Delete Previous Next Addresses

From: smartsearch@adhunter.co.uk
Date: 07 December
To:
Subject: Search Results from Fish4

This is your search for a job vacancy from Fish4Jobs.

You were looking for : Journalist.
Register reference : agt_218355_sits.
Search initiated on : 02-12
Search terminates on : 16-12
This search has produced 2 results shown below.

---

1. Journalist Journalism Wee Country Publishing Stirlingshire Journalist Vacancy An opportunity has arisen for a Journalist to join the staff of the Wee County News, Clackmannanshire's award winning weekly newspaper which is printed web offset with full colour facilities. The successful applicant will be qualified to and possess an NCTJ certificate and have a minimum of one years experience on a local paper. A good news sense, a nose for a story and the ability to work under pressure, good shorthand, experience of court/local council coverage. A working knowledge of QuarkXpress would be an advantage.

Figure 4.2 Many papers and agencies will e-mail details of jobs that match your search criteria at `www.fish4jobs.co.uk`

Employment agencies have always made passive job search possible. They store your CV and contact you with suitable vacancies. Most now do a substantial proportion of their recruitment through the Web in ways that can take some of the hard work out of job hunting.

Some employers invite detailed speculative applications that are stored for a set period and matched against vacancies as they occur. 'We'll keep you on file' really means something with employers like Hewlett Packard who retain your electronic CV as an active application for six months.

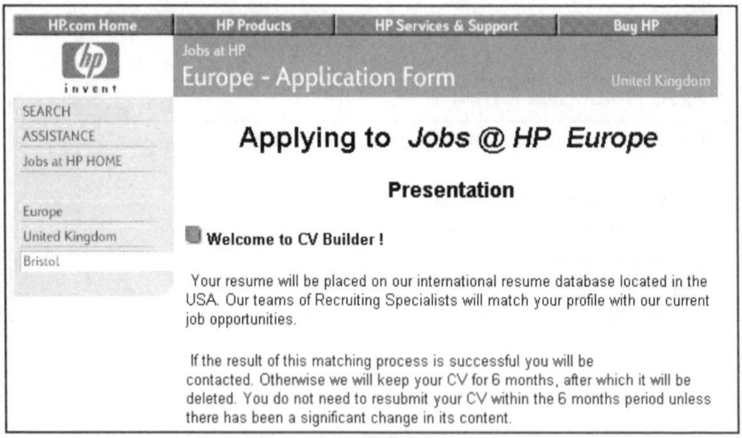
HP.com Home
HP Products
HP Services & Support
Buy HP
invent
Jobs at HP
Europe - Application Form
United Kingdom
SEARCH
ASSISTANCE
Jobs at HP HOME
Europe
United Kingdom
Bristol
Applying to Jobs @ HP Europe
Presentation
Welcome to CV Builder !
Your resume will be placed on our international resume database located in the USA. Our teams of Recruiting Specialists will match your profile with our current job opportunities.
If the result of this matching process is successful you will be contacted. Otherwise we will keep your CV for 6 months, after which it will be deleted. You do not need to resubmit your CV within the 6 months period unless there has been a significant change in its content.

Figure 4.3 One application does for all jobs for six months with HP at `www.jobs.hp.com`

There are degrees of passivity. Registering with newspaper sites like Jobs Unlimited or Fish4it takes very little thought or effort. You select job criteria through a series of dropdown menus. In return vacancies that match your specified choices will be selected and in some cases e-mailed to you. This will not get you a job, but will prevent you missing an advert that you might like to investigate further. With employers, you need to put considerable effort into making an initial application even if it is speculative. Employment agencies come somewhere in between. Their registration forms are not usually as demanding as those of employers, but detailed enough to enable more specific matching than the newspaper sites.

Job search done in this way can yield good results disproportionate to the effort invested. It is particularly useful for those who have little time for advert scanning, are geographically mobile, want a job in another area or country or are vaguely thinking about changing jobs and want to see what's out there without spending too long over it.

Active job hunting

If you're after a job sooner rather than later, you need to look actively for additional vacancies. The easiest to find are those that are advertised. Examples of sites for these are at the end of this chapter.

In addition to giving access to advertised vacancies, the Web can help you make non-intrusive contact with employers. If you are really keen to work for a particular company, but there are no vacancies when you first contact them, you may be reluctant to try again every day for six-months. That could be one way of making certain they never offer you an interview! However, only contacting them at six-weekly intervals could mean you miss the opportunity to apply for your dream job. If you look at their Web site every day, you won't be causing a nuisance, and yet you will be certain to see the vacancy when it occurs. The BBC, for example, encourages this approach by suggesting you add the page where jobs that interest you appear to **Favorites** and visit regularly.

Look out for recruitment fairs. They're an easy way to meet employers looking for staff. Magazines, newspapers and recruitment sites often sponsor such events; *The Guardian* is good for graduate recruitment fairs (see Figure 5.13), the *Caterer and Hotelkeeper's* 'Events' section has details of events for the hospitality industry and other specialist publications do something similar.

CV banks and databases

Newspaper sites like Revolver, see page 84, and most employment agencies offer the facility for you to register a CV with them for a specified amount of time. It is then made available to employers.

> Your CV is normally treated as confidential information and should not show personal details without your authorization.

With reputable agencies your privacy is protected and there is a clear statement of their privacy policy. There is usually the option to deny access to certain employers – useful if you don't want your current employer to see you're looking for a new job. You could choose to display your CV on your own Web site, but the chances of the right employers finding it may be minimal and you should be careful about making personal details so freely available; agencies protect your privacy. See Chapter 5 for details on preparing your CV for inclusion on agency sites and for speculative applications.

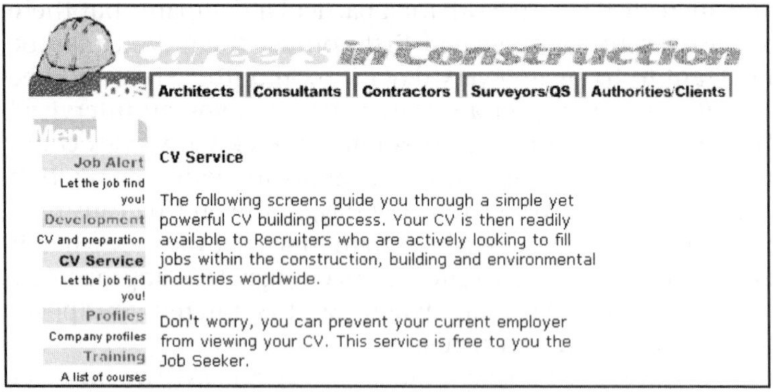

Figure 4.4 CV databases can give you a lot of exposure and protect your privacy at the same time at `www.careersinconstruction.com`

Speculative applications

Since the majority of vacancies are not publicly advertised, a well researched, speculative application can yield good results. Company information on the Web is presented in a way that makes it easy to identify and research potential jobs. Almost any Web site you look at has details of employment opportunities. Next time you go to your ISP's home page, to book a holiday or buy a book, check out whether they're looking for staff and if what they've got on offer could appeal to you (see Figure 4.12).

Many employers positively encourage speculative application via their site. Even if they don't mention recruitment they'll still provide information you can use to help convince them they need you.

As the number of companies with Web sites increases, so does the opportunity to be more creative with your job search.

Making a speculative application does not mean sending your basic CV to any employer on the offchance that there is something suitable. The research for such an application needs to be more detailed than one for a job that exists. You are aiming to show an employer that there is a need you can meet, when they didn't even know they had it. For help with constructing an effective CV, see Chapter 5.

THE BEST PLACES TO LOOK

Newspapers and journals

Newspapers are traditionally the first place jobseekers look for vacancies. They are an excellent source of focused information. Local newspapers cover defined geographical areas, national papers often specialize on occupational sectors on different days of the week. The Web has made newspapers all over the world easily and, in most cases, freely accessible. Sites that link to electronic newspapers and journals from around the world can be found on page 82.

Many newspapers have developed online vacancy databases. As they derive a substantial part of their revenue from advertising jobs, Web-based resources enhance the service they offer to employers. Comprehensive information to support an advert is often the key to an employer getting the sort of response they want. It would be prohibitively expensive to include detailed job descriptions in newspaper adverts, but on a Web site the advert can include links to everything an applicant needs to know. If it's clear what an employer's requirements are, applicants are more likely to self-select. Many newspaper adverts include links to employer sites. Where these provide self-selection tools they save both applicant and employer a lot of wasted time and effort.

The vacancy sections of newspapers and journals usually allow you to conduct job-specific searches based on keyword matching or browse for jobs by type of work, location and salary range.

Many have additional resources, including careers advice, e-mail notification and organizational tools that make life easier. This type of service is offered by local as well as national newspapers.

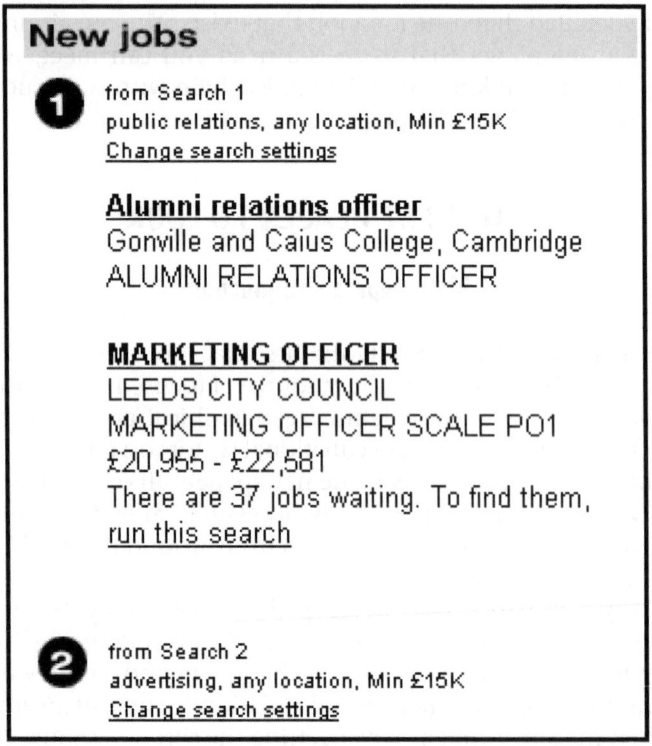

New jobs
1
from Search 1
public relations, any location, Min £15K
Change search settings
Alumni relations officer
Gonville and Caius College, Cambridge
ALUMNI RELATIONS OFFICER
MARKETING OFFICER
LEEDS CITY COUNCIL
MARKETING OFFICER SCALE PO1
£20,955 - £22,581
There are 37 jobs waiting. To find them, run this search
2
from Search 2
advertising, any location, Min £15K
Change search settings

Figure 4.5 Jobs Unlimited's Career Manager saves you having to re-enter your search details each time you visit the site at **www.jobsunlimited.co.uk**

Professional and trade journals are a good source of vacancy information in specialist fields. There's one for every occupation from architecture to zoology and the number with Web sites is growing. In addition to vacancies, these sites give access to details of news, research and concerns affecting their profession. Invaluable for pre-application research.

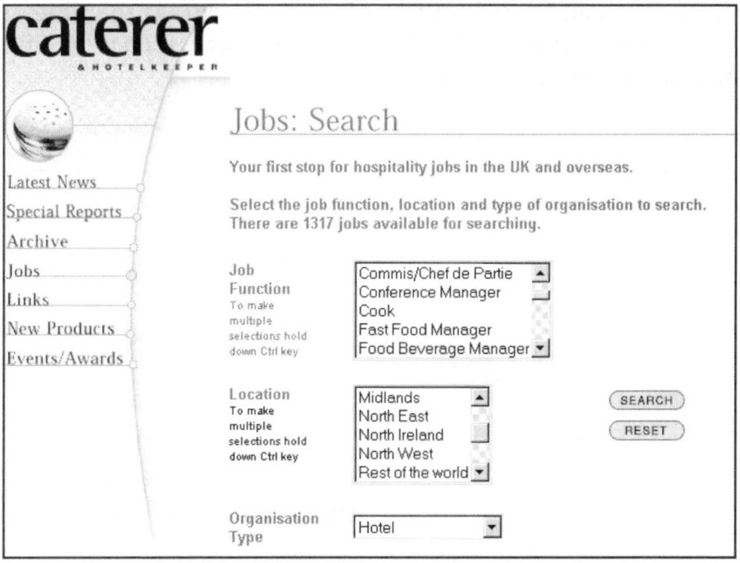

Figure 4.6 Specialist magazines are a focused resource for job search at `www.caterer.com`

Employment agencies

Employment agencies aim to fill posts quickly with the best person available. They have two customers, the employer and the applicant. To meet the demands of both they must provide accurate, up-to-date information. Many provide extra assistance to applicants with applying for jobs, researching employers, preparing for interviews and selection tests. Some have detailed careers information, current labour market information and links to discussion groups on job-search related topics.

Employment agencies were quick to see and utilize the potential of the Web. It enables them to offer employers a huge bank of potential applicants. Some advertise vacancies applicants can search; some keep a bank of CVs for employers to choose from (see Figure 4.7). Agencies are often asked to carry out an initial screening of applicants and prevent employers being overwhelmed by the response. Some agencies have been unscrupulous about helping themselves to vacancies posted elsewhere on the Web and passing them off as their own. At the time of writing the Department for Trade and Industry (DTI) is looking at making this an offence.

Figure 4.7 Monster offers a range of resources and services to make finding and getting a job easier at **`www.monster.co.uk`**

Most agencies on the Web are commercial organizations, but state employment agencies also make use of this technology. The UK Employment Services will offer all Job Centre vacancies and additional job hunting resources on their site **`www.employmentservice.gov.uk`** from the end of 2000. The EURES site described later in this chapter gives access to all state employment agencies in Europe, most of which make their vacancies available online.

Employers

The Web allows employers to reach a huge audience without using intermediaries such as newspapers and agencies. It's a cheap and effective way to target computer-literate applicants who are demonstrating their motivation, initiative and confidence in the use of new technologies by searching for vacancies in this way.

> Increasing numbers of employers are moving to direct recruitment using their own Web sites.

Most employers regard the increased number of applicants which their Web presence generates as a positive development. However, in the same way that unlimited vacancies can cause problems for jobseekers, unlimited applications can cause problems for employers. Many employers incorporate self-selection exercises into their sites to encourage focused and thoughtful applications. GCHQ, for example, invite potential applicants to show their talent for spotting encoded information by taking the 'GCHQ Challenge' before they apply.

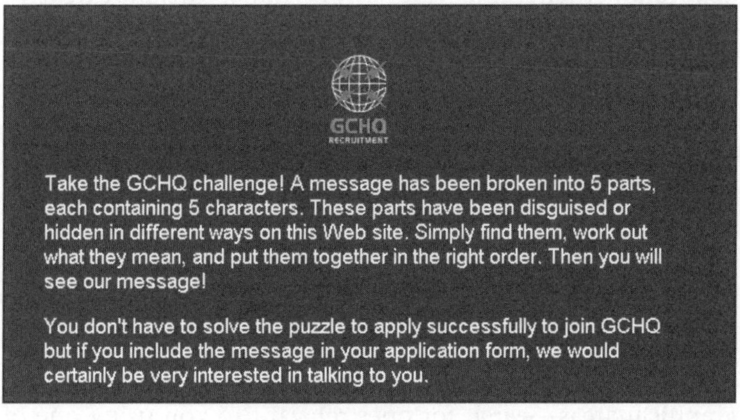

Figure 4.8 An unusual but effective approach to self selection at `www.gchq.gov.uk`

The ease of electronic communication should not tempt you to fire off multiple, ill-researched applications to all and sundry. Many companies use their Web site to provide detailed information on themselves, their vacancies and what they require of employees. They do this to help applicants be more realistic about positions they apply for. Where an employer goes to the bother of maintaining a Web site there will also be an expectation that you have used it effectively. Employers report frustration at receiving e-mail queries on matters fully covered on their site. Asking questions that show you have not bothered to research your application properly, or that you have problems understanding written information, will not enhance your prospects of getting a job (see Figure 4.9).

Employers use their sites to encourage applications in a variety of ways. Some advertise specific vacancies and provide online forms. In many cases these are initially evaluated by screening software (see page 117). Looking at a range of employer sites can be useful, as the hints and tips each offers can help with other applications.

Employers who use the Web as a recruitment tool without advertising specific vacancies give general company information and details such as recruitment procedures, entry requirements and employee profiles. These give valuable insight into the range of skills and other attributes they want to see highlighted in an application. KPMG and Unilever, for example, include extensive recruitment information on their site without advertising specific vacancies. They have found that this results in fewer requests for application packs, but a higher proportion of those requesting packs is suitable for the posts they are targeting. Many companies that recruit new graduates take this approach on their Web sites.

Newsgroups

These are an additional source of vacancy information. Some deal with specific career areas, others concentrate on geographical areas. Search for ones relevant to you using one of the search engines dedicated to newsgroups such as:
`www.deja.com/usenet`
or use the ready-made links from Career Mosaic.

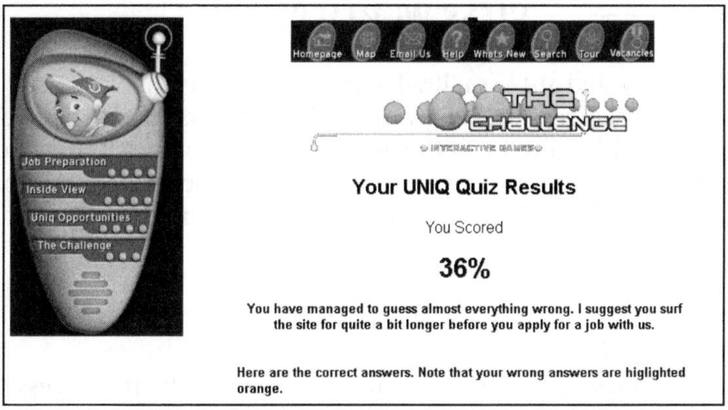

Figure 4.9 Save yourself embarrassment at interview by researching any employer you're applying to thoroughly at `uniq.unilever.com`

The sheer number of vacancies on the Web could lead you to believe that all jobs are advertised there. That is not the case. Some jobs are advertised only on the Web, a growing number on the Web and elsewhere at the same time and many by a variety of time-honoured methods, such as word of mouth and networking. Effective job search calls for a combination of old and new methods.

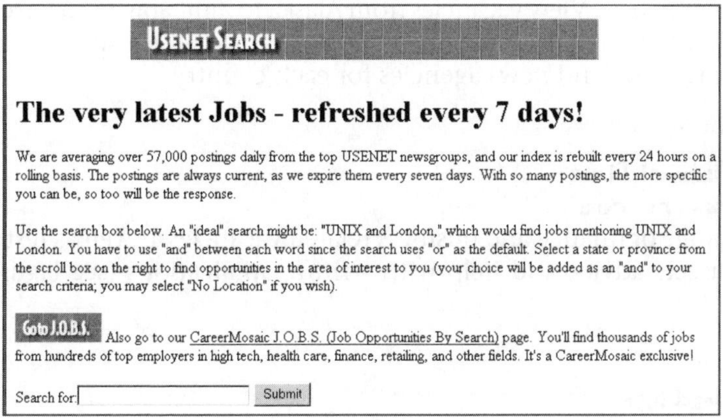
USENET SEARCH
The very latest Jobs - refreshed every 7 days!
We are averaging over 57,000 postings daily from the top USENET newsgroups, and our index is rebuilt every 24 hours on a rolling basis. The postings are always current, as we expire them every seven days. With so many postings, the more specific you can be, so too will be the response.
Use the search box below. An "ideal" search might be: "UNIX and London," which would find jobs mentioning UNIX and London. You have to use "and" between each word since the search uses "or" as the default. Select a state or province from the scroll box on the right to find opportunities in the area of interest to you (your choice will be added as an "and" to your search criteria; you may select "No Location" if you wish).
Goto J.O.B.S.
Also go to our CareerMosaic J.O.B.S. (Job Opportunities By Search) page. You'll find thousands of jobs from hundreds of top employers in high tech, health care, finance, retailing, and other fields. It's a CareerMosaic exclusive!
Search for:
Submit

Figure 4.10 Career Mosaic provides a link to jobs-related newsgroups via their site at `www.careermosaic-uk.co.uk`

SITES WORTH SEEING

The sites listed are a small selection of what's available. They've been chosen to show the range of employers using the Web and to highlight some of the innovative methods used to attract and inform applicants. Many of the sites described at the end of Chapter 3 also have current vacancy information.

Newspapers

All the newspapers and journals listed below offer free access to vacancies, although most ask you to register.

E&P Directory of Online Newspapers
`www.emedia1.mediainfo.com/emedia`
Claims to be the most comprehensive reference resource of its kind. Papers with online editions are listed by country or you can search for specific publications, locations or attributes.

Kidon Media-Link
`www.kidon.com/media-link`
This Dutch site has listings of and links to all the world's major newspapers. View vacancies from Alaska to Zimbabwe and check the weather at the same time. There are links to television, radio, magazines and news agencies for each country.

Financial Times
`www.ft.com`
Range of finance and business related vacancies as well as tests, careers advice and help with writing applications (see Figure 4.11).

Fish4Jobs
`www.fish4jobs.co.uk`
A compilation of vacancies from the UK's regional press. Claims to give access to tens of thousands of vacancies that are updated

daily. Search profiles are matched against vacancies and details can be e-mailed daily for a fixed period (see Figures 4.2 and 4.12). Covers all regions of the UK.

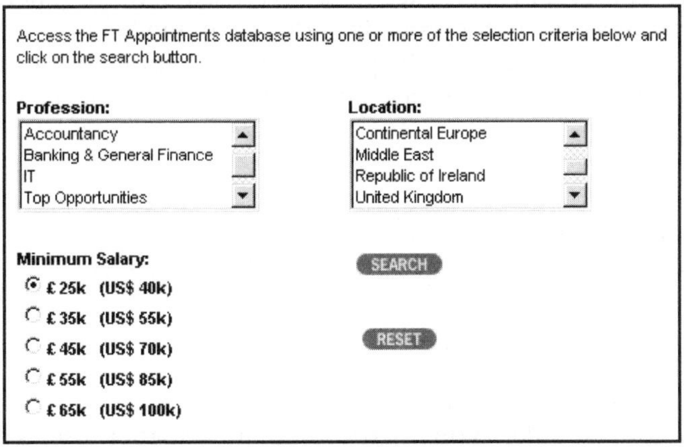

Figure 4.11 Nothing below £25k here at `www.ft.com`

Figure 4.12 Even the people who advertise jobs have jobs on offer

The Guardian

`www.jobsunlimited.co.uk`

The search facility allows selection by a range of criteria, including location and salary. Vacancies advertised here are generally of a professional nature covering education, media, marketing, IT, the environment and the public service. Explore the 'Career Manager' section, it can save a lot of time (see Figure 4.5).

Irish Times

`www.ireland.com`

Searchable site for jobs advertised in *The Irish Times*.

The Times

`www.the-times.co.uk`

This address takes you to the main newspaper site. Their appointments Web site is at **`www.revolver.com`**. Browse or search for all jobs advertised in *The Times* and *Sunday Times* or register to have matching vacancies sent by e-mail. Jobs advertised cover a range of professions; detailed job descriptions include a link to the employer's site. The papers' own vacancies are supplemented with ones from selected agencies and once you've found the job to apply for there's all the help you need with applications and interviews. Explore the 'Workstyle' section for thought-provoking articles on all aspects of working life.

Workthing

`www.workthing.com`

From The Guardian Media Group, but with different vacancies from those found in the paper and on Jobs Unlimited. Use the Matrix to search vacancies by sector, role, location and salary.

Professional and trade journals

British Medical Journal

`www.bmj.com`

Free registration gives you access to a wide range of medical vacancies in the UK and elsewhere.

The Caterer and Hotelkeeper

www.caterer.com

The online version of this well-known magazine has over a thousand vacancies for chefs, conference managers, hotel porters, hotel managers, maids, housekeepers, receptionists and wine waiters.

Computer Weekly

www.computerweekly.co.uk

Database of jobs and a jobs-by-e-mail service. Useful careers advice section and a salary checker based on analyses of advertisements for computer professionals.

Careers in Construction

www.careersinconstruction.com

Current vacancies, a CV service and e-mail alert for new vacancies take the hard work out of job hunting for a professional career in construction (see Figure 4.4).

Dalton's Weekly

www.daltons.co.uk

Specializes in the sale of businesses in the UK and overseas. Includes shops, residential care premises, pubs and clubs, catering businesses, hotels, guesthouses and franchises.

Estates Gazette

www.egi.co.uk

Careers advice, vacancy database, e-mail alerts and salary information for jobs in property.

Flight International

www.flightinternational.com (see Figure 4.13)

Health Service Journal

www.hsj.co.uk

Weekly UK health policy and management magazine. Vacancies for medical, nursing, social work, research, personnel, health promotion and management.

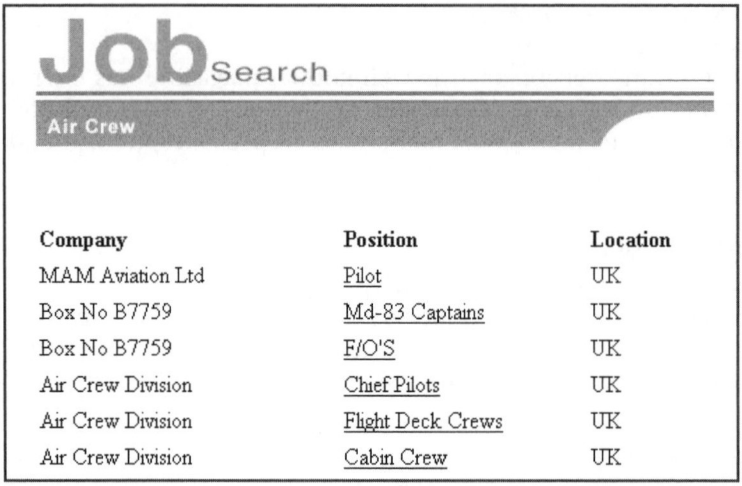
Job Search

Air Crew

Company	Position	Location
MAM Aviation Ltd	Pilot	UK
Box No B7759	Md-83 Captains	UK
Box No B7759	F/O'S	UK
Air Crew Division	Chief Pilots	UK
Air Crew Division	Flight Deck Crews	UK
Air Crew Division	Cabin Crew	UK

Figure 4.13 Current vacancies for all flight-related jobs, including cabin crew, flight deck and engineering staff

In Brief

`www.inbrief.co.uk`

This 500-page Web site keeps you updated on key legal events and issues in the UK and worldwide. It carries a selection of In Brief's lead stories from the current month's issue. It has a searchable appointments section and a 'Bluffers Guide' to London firms that aims to give an insider's perspective to a selection of law firms.

Local Government Chronicle

`www.lgcnet.com`

Comprehensive listing of local authority jobs updated weekly. Vacancies can be searched for by job type, employer type, or salary level. Additional resources include profiles of employers, detailed job descriptions and downloadable application forms.

Marketing Online

`www.marketing.haynet.com`

Weekly listing of a wide range of marketing jobs. 'Careerfiles' providing extensive corporate information are free for companies who have advertised in *Marketing* magazine in the previous four weeks.

Nature

www.nature.com

Details of international science jobs updated weekly. Vacancies are listed by subject, country, organization or position. There are links to employer profiles and details of conferences and fellowships.

New Scientist

www.newscientist.com

The recruitment database offers approximately three hundred UK scientific, technological and academic vacancies a week. Search is by employment category, discipline and keywords and there's a database of studentships.

Physics World Jobs

www.physicsweb.org/jobs

Part of the UK's Institute of Physics site. Regularly updated information on jobs and research opportunities. There are plans to merge PhysicsJobs and TIPTOP Jobs together to form the most comprehensive global physics jobs directory in the world (see Figure 4.14).

Therapy Weekly

www.therapy.co.uk

Jobs advertised in the magazine are searchable online including a range of occupations allied to medicine such as physiotherapy, dietetics, speech therapy and occupational therapy. Vacancies for play, drama and art therapy also appear here.

Times Educational Supplement

www.jobs.tes.co.uk

The weekly publication for teachers in primary, secondary and further education has all its vacancies on this site. Jobs can be

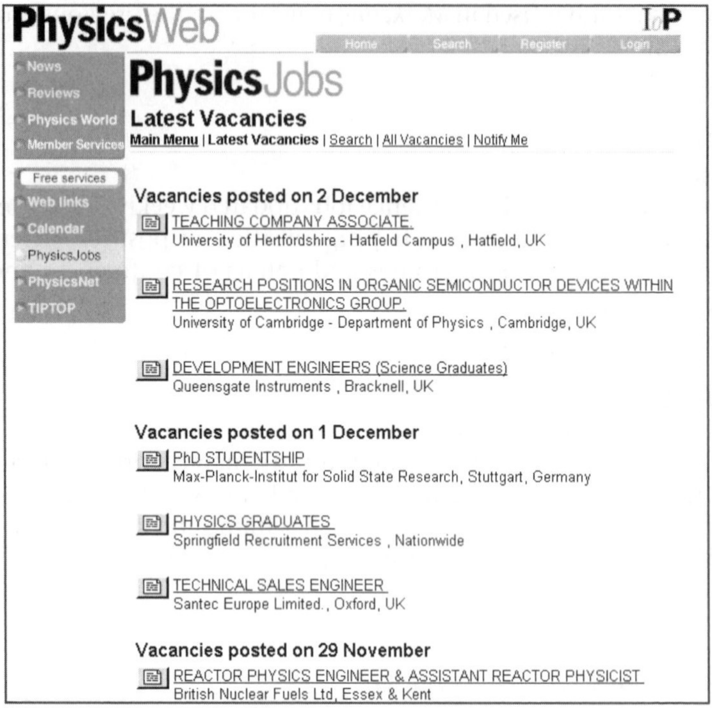

Figure 4.14 A career in physics can start here

viewed online or you can subscribe to an e-mail alert service. To read the main paper go to www.tes.co.uk.

The Times Higher Education Supplement provides a similar service for jobs in universities at www.jobs.thes.co.uk. The main paper is at www.thesis.co.uk (see Figure 4.15).

The Stage

www.thestage.co.uk

Vacancies for actors and those in related professions. Job listings are updated weekly and organized into sixteen categories, including acting, cruise work, dancing, backstage work and production. The 'Connect' section of the site has a range of articles to help you plan a career in the entertainment industry.

Figure 4.15 Make life easier for yourself and help out a friend

Employment agencies

The headline figures for the number of vacancies on some of these sites can be daunting, but don't be put off. Many agencies share listings, or help themselves to each other's in an attempt to make their store of jobs appear the largest. Nevertheless they are a good resource for finding jobs to apply for and most offer information on application and interview techniques, labour market and salary trends.

Academic jobs

www.jobs.ac.uk

Database of academic jobs in the UK. Look through recent vacancies or have jobs that match your requirements e-mailed to you every week. Site includes detailed profiles of employers.

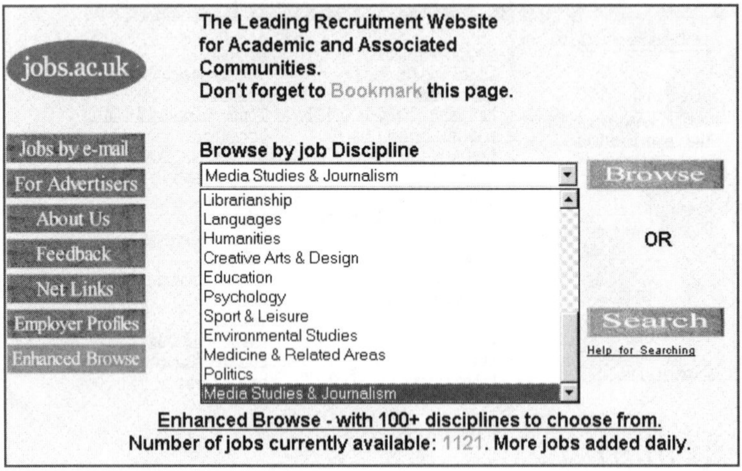

Figure 4.16 Browse or have vacancies sent by e-mail

Capita RAS

www.rasnet.co.uk

The recruitment agency for the Civil Service. Current vacancies are displayed and include a huge variety of posts such as buyers for the prison service, ecologists, quantity surveyors, secretaries and immigration officers.

Career Mosaic

www.careermosaic-uk.co.uk

Described as 'reshaping the job finding process', Career Mosaic has separate sites for different parts of the world. There's a database of jobs, the facility to post your CV online, a searchable index of newsgroups for jobseekers and employers' profiles.

The Career Resource Centre gives advice on CVs, covering letters and interviews.

Citizens First

www.citizens.eu

A comprehensive resource for investigating employment opportunities in Europe. Enter your country of origin and the country you want to work in for a range of information including comparability of professional qualifications. Printed material can be downloaded or ordered online.

Cool Works

www.coolworks.com

Described as a 'labor of love' by its creator Bill Berg, who works from his home in Yellowstone National Park, the site provides links to details of jobs in 'Great Places'. These include National and State Parks, cruise ships to Alaska, ski resorts and ranches. Just looking at the site is enough to give you itchy feet! Most of the work is seasonal. Non-US residents generally require a J1 visa. Details of this for UK residents are on the US Embassy site in the 'Visa Services' section at www.usembassy.org.uk.

EURES – European Employment Service

www.europa.eu.int/jobs/eures

Excellent resource for finding vacancies or information on living and working conditions in Europe. There are links to the public employment services in all EU and EEA member states. Check current vacancies anywhere from Greece to Iceland and explore the implications of living and working there (see Figure 4.17).

Gis-a-Job

www.gisajob.com

One of the first employment agencies to make use of mobile phone internet access. Jobs cover sectors such as IT, media, retail and tourism. Browse through vacancies, arrange to have them sent by e-mail or make your CV available.

Job Site

www.jobsite.co.uk

Created in 1995, Jobsite claims to have over 40,000 vacancies every month from 35 industry sectors including sales, marketing,

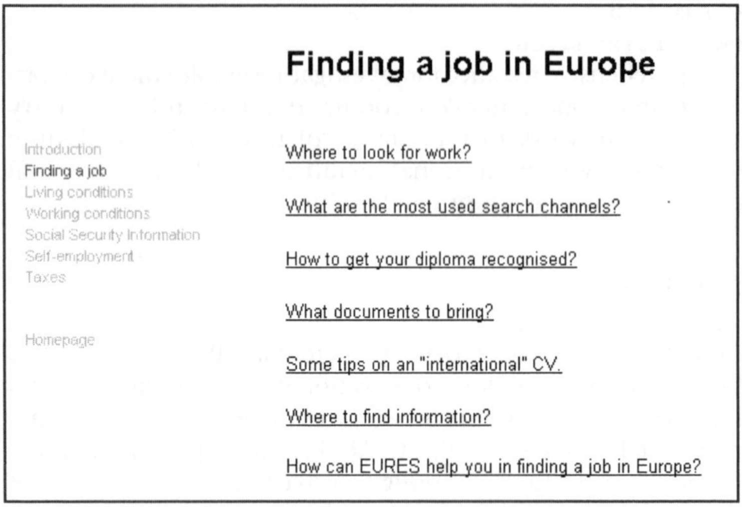

Figure 4.17 Explore the possibilities

management, accountancy, secretarial and administration, IT, telecommunications and engineering. There's a database of jobs, e-mail notification, the facility to store a CV and covering letter and useful advice on all stages of the job-hunting process.

The Monster Board

`www.monster.co.uk`

Monster have been around for some time in the world of online employment agencies and their site has an impressive range of facilities supplementing the job search service. As well as browsing for jobs or having them sent by e-mail there are employer profiles, interactive interview help, CV tips, a weekly newsletter and 'Ask the Expert' sections.

People Bank

`www.peoplebank.com`

Search for jobs or submit your CV for employers to find. Personal details are kept confidential and the initial contact is handled by the agency.

Price Jamieson

`www.pricejam.co.uk`

Specialize in new media, media marketing and communications recruitment. Browse through available jobs or register your CV and wait to be notified of suitable vacancies.

Taps

`www.taps.com`

A wide range of employers uses this agency including the BBC, British Air Traffic Control and major scientific, IT and large manufacturing companies. When you apply for a job advertised on the database, your previously registered CV is automatically sent to that employer. CV details are kept confidential and can only be looked at by the individual they belong to and TAPs' staff. Lots of useful related links and magazine type features on the labour market.

Total Jobs

`www.totaljobs.com`

Reed Business Publications, who produce a range of trade and professional journals, are behind this site. Use it to find current vacancies in aerospace, optometry, catering, property, construction, retail, electronics, social care, human resources and travel.

Wide Eyes

`www.wideeyes.com`

Hoping to revolutionize the recruitment market, Wide Eyes focus on competence rather than qualifications. The registration process for this site is lengthy but illuminating. Jobseekers are given the opportunity to complete online personality and emotional intelligence questionnaires as well as a range of very detailed information on their ambitions, experience, education and skills. The company has 26 Web sites in 12 languages and aims to think globally but act locally (see Figure 5.9).

The following selection of smaller, specialist agencies is included as a guide to the diversity of opportunities advertised on the Web.

Active Connection

`www.activeconnection.co.uk`

Recruitment agency for the leisure, fitness and beauty industry.

Aupair JobMatch

`www.aupairs.co.uk`

Searchable database of families requiring au pairs. Jobseekers can search by the country in which they want to work and nationality of family. Site can be viewed in English, Swedish, German, Portuguese or French.

Figure 4.18 Opportunities are available all over the world

Capital Markets Consulting Ltd

`www.cmcx.com`

Discover what investment bankers do, search for current vacancies or make use of the discreet vacancy notification service.

Charity People

www.charitypeople.co.uk

The not-for-profit sector employs thousands of people. The diverse range of organizations share a common goal – the desire to improve the world. This agency specializes in recruiting for the sector. The jobs advertised are varied and cover all business activities.

Digitext

www.digitext.co.uk

Specialist agency for technical authors.

FÁS – Training & Employment Authority (Ireland)

www.fas.ie

Access to all employment services vacancies in the Republic of Ireland. These can be searched by occupation, location or date posted.

FoodJobs

www.foodjobs.co.uk

Specializes in vacancies in food manufacturing and associated industries. Jobs advertised include marketing, management, finance, product development, scientific and engineering positions.

International Guild of Professional Butlers and Private Personnel Ltd

www.butlersguild.com

Contains a selection of surprisingly well-paid vacancies for chauffeurs, caretakers, butlers, handymen and chambermaids. Members have access to a wider range of vacancies and are notified of ones that meet their criteria (see Figure 4.19).

Public Sector Recruitment

www.psr-agency.com

Specializes in public sector jobs. These range from care assistants and gardeners to computer engineers and managers. See Figure 4.1.

➡ **Position:**	➡ **Free Time & Vacation:**
Female Butler / Housekeeper / Household Manager	2 days off per week, 30 days paid vacation per year.
➡ **Location:**	➡ **Starting Date:**
PARIS / FRANCE	OCTOBER / NOVEMBER
➡ **Client:**	➡ **Requirements:**
Private family from Saudi Arabia. The client spends no more than 30 to 60 days per year at this home.	The client is looking for a female because of the cultural aspects, a lady who can work alone and who does not mind being by herself most of the year. Languages: fluent French and English.
➡ **Salary:**	➡ **Duties:**
Excellent	Cleaning, serving, organizing, managing etc. A to Z, no other staff.
➡ **Housing:**	➡ **Position Quality:**
Included	The BEST. Long-term position.
➡ **Car:**	➡ **Medical & Dental Insurance:**
Not included	Included, + Pension Benefits + Bonus scheme.

Figure 4.19 There's everything you need to know about being a butler on this site

Recruitment & Employment Confederation (REC)

`www.rec.uk.com`

REC sets standards for how agencies operate. Use their site to check what you need to look out for when you sign up with an employment agency. The site gives full details of how agencies should operate, as well as listings of and links to member companies.

TEFL Professional Network

www.tefl.com

Describes itself as the world's most popular source of international English language teaching jobs. As well as a good range of vacancies to browse through, there are e-mail notification, a free newsletter and a CV database.

Thomas Telford Recruitment

www.t-telford.co.uk

The official recruitment consultancy of the Institution of Civil Engineers and the Institution of Chemical Engineers.

Young Scientist

www.young-scientist.co.uk

Specializes in laboratory vacancies with UK companies. Vacancies range from school leaver level to management positions. The emphasis is on those seeking their first or second appointment.

UK Employment Service

www.employmentservice.gov.uk

All vacancies notified to Job Centres will be available on the internet Job Bank that will be part of a wider 'Learning and Work Bank'.

Employers

The sites of many employers, large and small, offer a wealth of careers information. What this may lack in impartiality is made up for by its accuracy and up-to-date content. The sites listed have been chosen to reflect the variety of what is available. Find employers' Web sites through one of the large business directories or a general search tool (see page 151).

For UK companies try the following:

The Biz

www.thebiz.co.uk

Company Annual Reports on Line

www.carol.co.uk

For US and global companies, look at these sites:

Hoover's Corporate Web Sites

www.hoovers.com

Hoover's has links to Web sites for more than 5,000 of the world's largest companies. It is possible to search just for those that have job listings.

Air 2000

www.air2000.ltd.uk

Details of ongoing recruitment for cabin crew, ground staff and customer service agents as well as administrative vacancies with the airline. If you're between 18 and 28 with two 'A' levels, preferably in sciences, and a passion for flying, look out for their pilot training scheme.

Andersen Consulting

www.careers.ac.com

Learn about the organization and opportunities it offers in management and technology consultancy. Search for opportunities by location or use the 'Career Profiler' to find current vacancies that match your abilities.

The Armed Forces

www.army.mod.uk

www.raf.mod.uk

www.royal-navy.mod.uk

All three armed forces have excellent Web sites with detailed recruitment, careers and sponsorship information. There are some excellent interactive features such as testing missions on the RAF site.

Asda

www.asda.co.uk

Take Asda's online quiz to see if you're suited to them.

BBC

www.bbc.co.uk

The 'World of Jobs' pages give details of current vacancies, links to detailed job descriptions, advice on application and in most cases the opportunity to apply online. The advice on applying highlights the need for candidates to show they have researched the area they are targeting. Their site contains all the necessary information.

British Airways

www.british-airways.com/inside/employme/employme.shtml

Vacancies advertised include cabin crew, information technology posts and sales jobs. There are also details of their pilot training programme.

BOND: British Overseas NGOs for Development

www.bond.org.uk

If you're looking for work that makes a difference to those in the developing world or some of its trouble spots, you'll find current vacancies here (see Figure 4.20).

The European Commission

www.cec.org.uk

Advertises the Commission's current vacancies for English speaking candidates. It has links to similar recruitment sites and agencies in other member states. Job descriptions are short but link to more detailed information.

Government Communications Headquarters (GCHQ)

www.gchq.gov.uk

If you want work that can have an impact on the political, military and economic well-being of the country take a look at

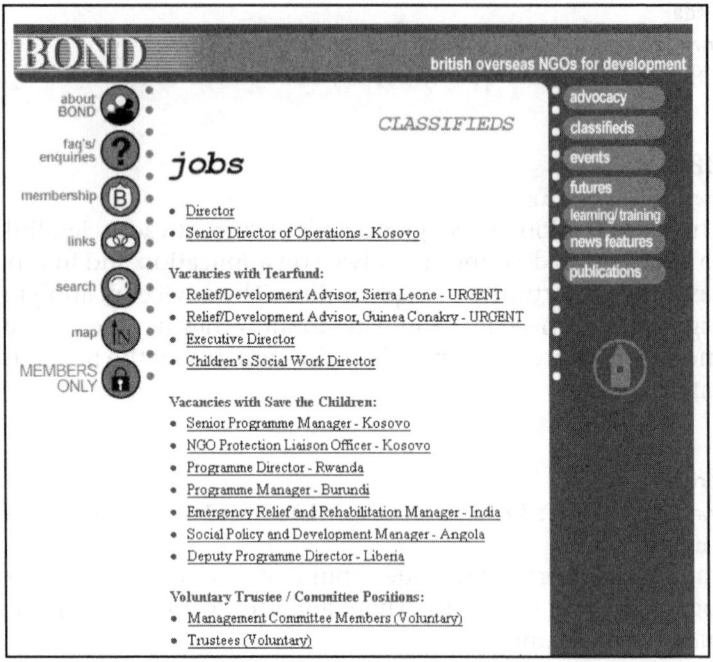

Figure 4.20 Looking for a different type of job satisfaction? Explore some of the opportunities with voluntary or not-for-profit organizations

this site. Career opportunities exist for linguists, mathematicians, administrators, librarians, technologists and graduate management trainees (see Figure 4.8).

Hewlett Packard

www.jobs.hp.com

Huge range of European vacancies updated daily. These are not limited to computing, but cover areas such as public relations, marketing, sales and accounts. Online and speculative application is encouraged. The company offer work experience to students who are invited to submit their own project idea. Learn about company culture by reading about the 'HP way' (see Figure 4.3).

KPMG

www.kpmg.co.uk

Specific vacancies are not advertised, but the site is used to encourage suitable final-year graduates to apply. The company provides a wealth of information and self-assessment tools to help applicants check their suitability.

MI5

www.mi5.gov.uk

No longer do you have to wait to be approached about a job in MI5, you can check out vacancies on their Web site. Opportunities exist for clerical and administrative staff, linguists, computer experts and intelligence officers.

Microsoft

www.microsoft.com/uk/jobs

Lots of jobs and information about the company in all of its different locations. Read case studies, apply online for current vacancies and student placements.

PriceWaterhouseCoopers

www.pwcglobal.com

UK's largest business advisory organization whose professional services include accounting and auditing, tax and consulting. Site has extensive careers information, graduate recruitment details and current vacancies, as well as detailed company and financial information.

Shell International

www.shell.com

Current vacancies are listed. The site search engine searches all Shell sites worldwide. Lots of company and careers information, employee profiles and links to all their other sites worldwide (see Figure 2.15).

SmithKlineBeecham

www.sb.com

Offers access to UK and US searches for current vacancies. These are for science, engineering, information technology and human resources graduates in both countries. A salaried industrial placement programme offers experience related to specific areas of academic interest for undergraduates.

Thomson's Holidays

www.thomson-holidays.com/jobs/jobs.htm

Thomson's recruit entertainment and children's representatives as well as general overseas staff. You need to be over 21 and have at least a year's experience of working with people in a customer service role before you complete the online application form.

Top Jobs

www.topjobs.co.uk

Employment agency that targets graduates and professionals. There is extensive help and advice on psychometric tests and the chance to complete online questionnaires to get you thinking about the things that really matter.

Unilever

www.uniq.unilever.com

Take advantage of the excellent information here to help prepare you for any job application or interview. Interactive games and problem solving exercises help you identify and articulate your skills. There's help with writing CVs, completing application forms, coping with selection tests and interviews (see Figure 4.9).

WORTH REMEMBERING

- The main sources of vacancy information are unchanged. However, they are made more accessible through the internet.
- Searching for vacancies on the Web should be quicker and more effective than using traditional means.
- It's easy to arrange to be notified of matching vacancies by e-mail.
- Many employers encourage speculative application through their Web sites.
- CV databases enable you to make your skills and abilities known to a large audience of potential employers.
- Try to use the same user name and password for sites you register with to make remembering them easier. Keep a record of user names and passwords.
- Web-based vacancy search should enhance, not replace, other means of job search.

5

APPLICATIONS AND INTERVIEWS

This chapter explains the techniques for making effective applications and shows how Web sites can help you with this and prepare you for the interview.

APPLICATION SKILLS

Current labour market trends mean that people are likely to apply for several jobs during their working life. The 'job for life' is no longer a reality for most, changing jobs or moving into a new career area is. Finding a job to apply for is easy compared to making an effective application for it. Communicating skills, potential and individuality, verbally or in writing, can be hard work. Putting the important and impressive things about yourself into words in a convincing way is daunting for most people.

With so much free help on the Web there's no need to sell yourself short because you don't know how to present CVs, application forms and covering letters.

On the whole we are brought up to be modest about ourselves. Having to communicate skills and abilities to strangers poses problems for many. One man's insecurity is another's business opportunity, and there are numerous ways in which you can part with money to get what is advertised as some magic formula for constructing applications that will secure the job you want.

Getting help with CV writing

A whole industry has grown up around advising how to compose CVs and covering letters. In some cases help is offered free of charge, in others for a fee. Good sources of free help include careers and employment centres, newspapers, educational broadcasters and employment agencies. They won't write your CV for you, but will help you construct it by providing detailed information including worksheets and examples. In some cases the material is produced by qualified guidance counsellors, based on research into the preferences and experiences of employers.

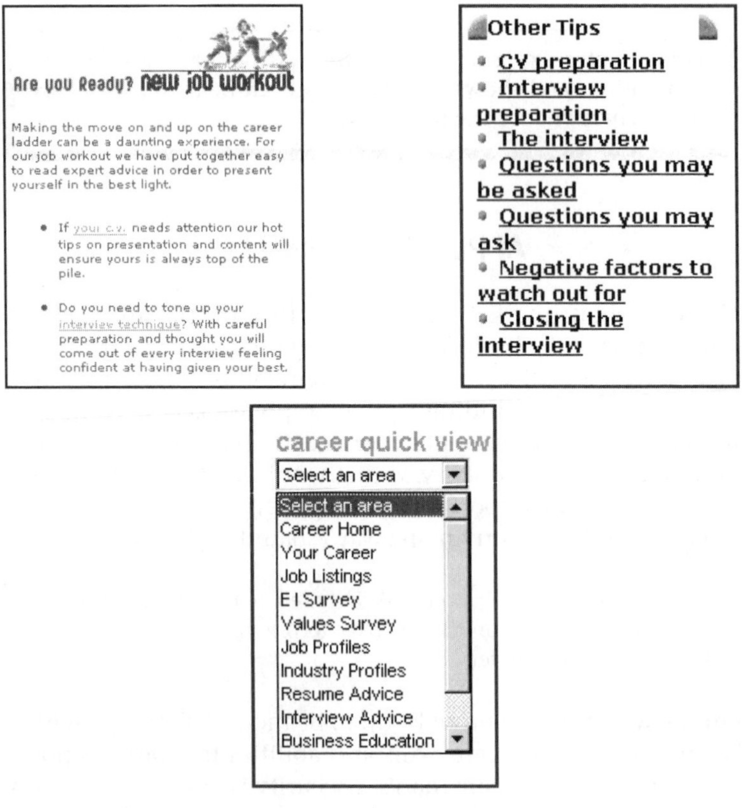

Figure 5.1 Web sites that advertise jobs usually have information to help you apply. These are from Active Challenge, *Computer Weekly* and the *Financial Times*

Fee-charging services usually compose and produce CVs. The quality of their product can vary from excellent to appalling. If you choose to pay for having your CV written, check the credentials of those who are doing it. Anyone can set up a Web site claiming to offer careers guidance and help with applications. Commercial companies offering a CV writing service are not featured here but can be found using a directory or search engine.

Writing your own CV

Constructing your own application is a valuable process to go through. If you have real trouble communicating about yourself, you are not going to do well at an interview. It is probably an indication that you are not yet ready to present yourself in a convincing way, but need to spend a little more time and effort on self-analysis, employer research or both.

In the end anything that is written about you is personal and should reflect the real you. A CV and covering letter do not get you a job; they get you an interview, where you have to live up to the expectations created by what you wrote. Employers are interested in **your** communication skills, not those of a commercial CV writing company.

> If your CV is slick and polished and you're not, the interviewers will be disappointed.

There are many places on and off the Web where you can get excellent practical help on style and format, essential content, employer preferences and other techniques needed to improve your application (see Figure 5.2). All the sites at the end of this chapter offer free, good quality advice.

CHOOSING THE RIGHT METHOD OF APPLICATION

Vacancies advertised on the Web may offer a choice of application methods and usually have clear instructions on each. Greater choice can mean greater potential for getting it wrong. It's important to follow the instructions provided by the employers about what they find acceptable and what their system copes with. As vacancies on the Web are accessible all over the world, take note of residency requirements. Don't waste your time applying for jobs where you will not be able to get a work permit or entry visa.

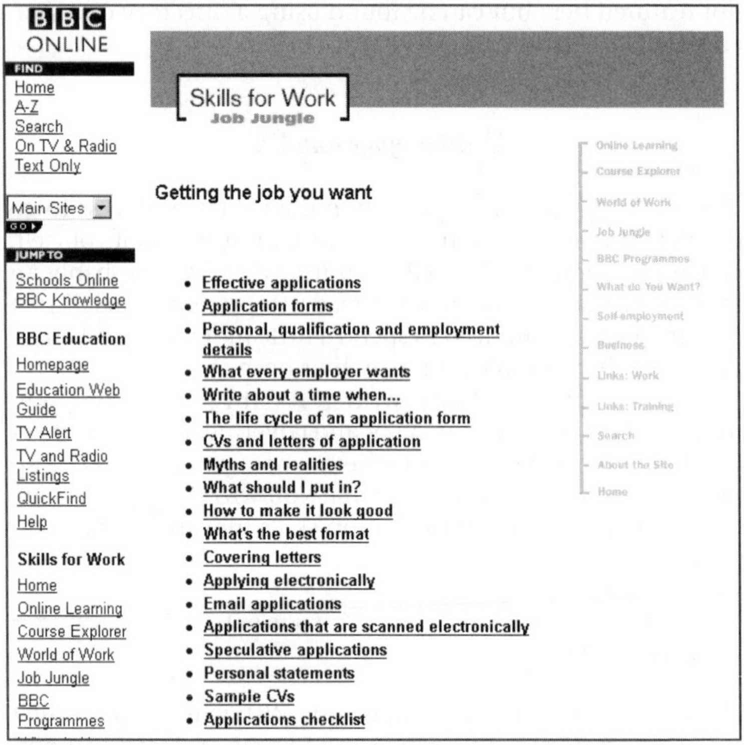

Figure 5.2 There's a lot of information available to help you write your own applications at `www.bbc.co.uk/education/workskills/jobs/index.shtml`

CV or application form?

Some employers offer the option of submitting a CV or completing their application form. With a CV you are in control of what you tell the employer and how you organize and present it. With an application form there are set questions to answer and spaces you have to fill. If there's a facility to apply online, copy and paste the form into a word processing package. Work on it with the same care you would lavish on any other application, then copy the details onto the original, print it out and read it again, before finally clicking the submit button.

An online application form should never be completed online initially.

Some recruitment sites provide a template that can be used for any application you make through their site (see Figure 5.3). The danger with this is that your application will not be targeted to each job you apply for. However, on most sites, stored forms can be accessed and modified to overcome this problem.

Welcome to Gradunet Application Forms
www.gradunet.co.uk/applications/
gradunet
ON-LINE APPLICATION FORM
PERSONAL ADMINISTRATION
Enter your login email address and unique password to access all your saved and completed Gradunet Application Forms.
Complete your Personal Profile and when you log in to other Gradunet Application Forms all your details will appear automatically

Figure 5.3 Gradunet takes some of the hard work out of completing forms

Electronic application

Developments in information technology have been introducing changes into application procedures for some time. Word processed CVs are the norm and many people send applications by e-mail. At the other end employers are increasingly using scanning software that reads forms electronically and does an initial selection based on keyword searches.

Where there is an option to apply electronically, either by completing an online form or e-mailing a CV and letter of application, you should take it. If an employer is advertising on the Web it means he or she wants someone who uses that medium. Applying electronically says in a most convincing way that you are computer literate and comfortable with new technologies. All employers look for communication skills and adaptability to change; this demonstrates both. Other advantages of applying electronically are:

- It makes all applications look the same. There is no need to agonize over choice of font, colour of paper, fancy formatting.
- It arrives in pristine condition.
- It is fast and can be sent at any time of the day.
- There are no distractions such as difficult-to-read handwriting or unusual signatures.

Completing application forms online does not allow you to leave blanks. Incomplete forms are not accepted for submission. Quite useful if you've accidentally forgotten to complete a section.

WRITING AN IMPRESSIVE CV

Five minutes after seeing the ideal job is not the best time to start composing your CV. Applications have closing dates which are always too soon if you need to start putting your details together from scratch. Your task at this stage should be to tailor the CV you constructed as part of your self-assessment exercises to the demands of this particular vacancy. This means changing the emphasis of certain sections and adapting its appearance and format to suit the way it is to be sent and received.

> Writing a CV is not a task you can do once and forget about. It will need constant change and adaptation. This can most easily be done if you have a strong framework.

Your basic CV could act as the one you use for registering with employment agencies and placing on CV banks. It will also form the raw material from which you fill in application forms and produce more targeted CVs. Avoid sending a CV you feel would do for any employer. Always include something that shows you have researched this post and this employer thoroughly. If you're applying for a job in another country, don't assume your standard CV layout will create the right impression.

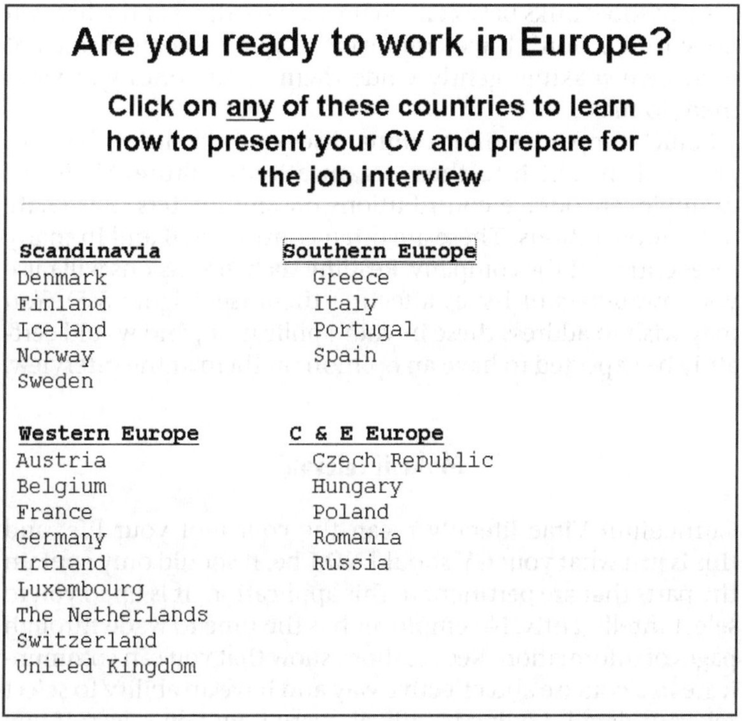

Are you ready to work in Europe?

Click on any of these countries to learn how to present your CV and prepare for the job interview

Scandinavia
Denmark
Finland
Iceland
Norway
Sweden

Southern Europe
Greece
Italy
Portugal
Spain

Western Europe
Austria
Belgium
France
Germany
Ireland
Luxembourg
The Netherlands
Switzerland
United Kingdom

C & E Europe
Czech Republic
Hungary
Poland
Romania
Russia

Figure 5.4 Eurograduate provides excellent information if you want to target overseas employers at **www.eurograduate.com**

Do your research

The secret of an excellent CV is excellent research – about you, the post and the employer. The skilled part is using this research to produce something that is concise, coherent and convincing. It's of prime importance to make it easy for the employer to understand how what you have done or learned in the past will enable you to do their work to a high standard.

Just listing your skills and interests is not enough. You need to provide concrete examples of how you successfully used those skills and the results you achieved.

Clearly show links between what you have done and what you hope to do. Don't leave employers to jump to conclusions of their own making, gently guide them to the ones you want them to make.

Some companies offer online discussion facilities that can give real insight into their organization's culture. Shell, for example, encourage contributions on any matters that relate to their operations. These are often controversial and in many cases critical of the company. Reading such discussions will raise your awareness of issues affecting them (see Figure 5.5). You may wish to address these in your application, and would certainly be expected to have an opinion on them at the interview.

Make it relevant

Curriculum Vitae literally mean the course of your life, and this is just what your CV should **NOT** be. It should only contain the parts that are pertinent to this application. It is up to you to select intelligently. No employer has the time to wade through pages of information. Keep it short, show that you can communicate in a concise and effective way and have an ability to select relevant detail. Look critically at every item you select; if you can't immediately see its relevance to the current objective, discard it. Your CV should arouse the readers' interest, not bore them to death (see Figure 5.6).

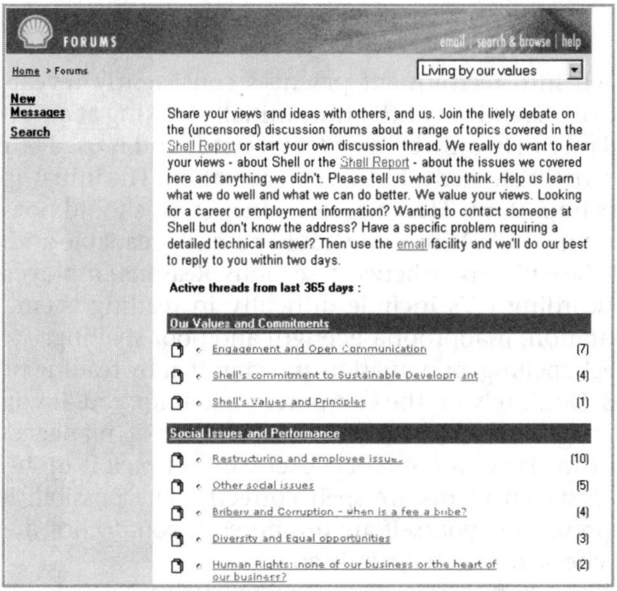

Figure 5.5 If you don't use all the resources an employer provides, you'll be at a disadvantage at `www.shell.com`

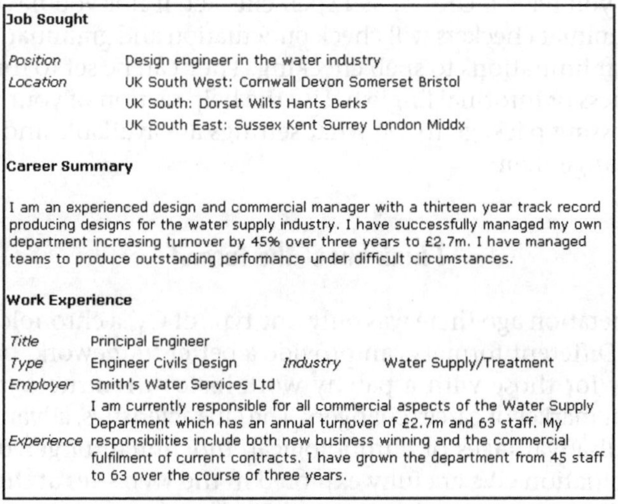

Job Sought

Position	Design engineer in the water industry
Location	UK South West: Cornwall Devon Somerset Bristol
	UK South: Dorset Wilts Hants Berks
	UK South East: Sussex Kent Surrey London Middx

Career Summary

I am an experienced design and commercial manager with a thirteen year track record producing designs for the water supply industry. I have successfully managed my own department increasing turnover by 45% over three years to £2.7m. I have managed teams to produce outstanding performance under difficult circumstances.

Work Experience

Title	Principal Engineer		
Type	Engineer Civils Design	*Industry*	Water Supply/Treatment
Employer	Smith's Water Services Ltd		
Experience	I am currently responsible for all commercial aspects of the Water Supply Department which has an annual turnover of £2.7m and 63 staff. My responsibilities include both new business winning and the commercial fulfilment of current contracts. I have grown the department from 45 staff to 63 over the course of three years.		

Figure 5.6 A sample CV from Careers in Construction at `www.careersinconstruction.com`

Concentrate on appearance and accuracy

Research into recruitment practices consistently reveals that employers spend very little time initially looking at a CV. Their first glance may only be for a few seconds and is used to determine whether it merits further consideration. The initial appearance is important. The quest for conciseness should not result in a cramped CV. Your font should be easily readable and there should be white space between sections. Reasons employers give for discarding CVs include difficulty in reading them, poor presentation, inappropriate length and poor spelling.

Check spelling, punctuation and grammar by reading printed copies. Don't rely on the computer to do it for you. If you type in 'managed teams of shifty corkers', instead of 'managed team of shift workers', the spell checker will not pick it up because your mistaken words are spelt correctly. The possibilities for misrepresenting yourself are unlimited if you do not meticulously check all you have written.

Spell checkers have language options such as English (US) and English (UK). Choose whichever is appropriate to the company. An easy way to see whether you are using UK or US English spelling is to check a word like 'color'. If it's highlighted as an error you have a UK English spell checker, if not you have US.

Grammar checkers will check punctuation and grammar, with similar limitations to spell checking. They can be set to formal, business or informal English. Use the help section of your word processing package to see what settings are available and how to change them.

Think about the format

A generation ago there was only one type of CV, a chronological one. Different formats can provide a better framework, particularly for those with a patchy work history, returnees to the labour market or career changers. The characteristics, advantages and disadvantages of chronological, functional, targeted and combination CVs are fully explored in the Web sites at the end of this chapter (see also Figure 5.7). The choice depends not only on your circumstances and employment history, but also on what you feel comfortable with.

Some employers can be suspicious of non-chronological CVs and regard them as trying to hide gaps in employment or study history. Others positively encourage applications that highlight skills gained through a range of experience.

CVs - Putting it all together

You've done all the hard work: you have done the self-analysis, you know what the employer is looking for and you have matched the two up... now it's time to get it down on paper!

Style

- Different styles of CV - Three common ways of laying out a CV.
- Let's get physical - How to ensure that when the recruiter picks up your CV, his first impression of you is a good one.
- Looking good on paper - Fonts, graphics, photographs... where to start AND when to stop!
- Putting your CV on the Internet - Guidelines for those who want to exploit the Web.

Figure 5.7 University careers service pages are full of advice on the application process at `www.netwise.ac.uk`

PRESENTATION HINTS

Whichever method of application you use, a basic understanding of what will happen to the words you write is important.

Paper CVs

The traditional paper CV that will not be scanned electronically will be scanned visually. How it looks is important and adds significantly to the first impression you create.

- Use paper of a reasonable quality. Heavy coloured paper is often an expensive distraction.
- Be aware that in the first instance it will only be glanced at. Consider what the first thing seen is. If it's your name, address, marital status, number of children, driving licence

details and qualifications from twenty years ago, it may not inspire the reader to look any further. If it's a concise summary of your skills, it will.

- Make use of formatting tools on word processing programs subtly. Bulleted lists are a good way of avoiding sentences always starting with the word 'I' and can look efficient. Use bold and underline where appropriate. They highlight the text, so be selective. If everything is highlighted, nothing stands out.
- Don't overdo borders and shading, neat and relatively plain can have more impact. This is not the place to show off your word processing skills.

CVs for electronic scanning

Employers using scanning software give clear guidelines on the format required. A CV accepted as worthy of further consideration by an electronic selector will then be looked at by a human one, so has to be attractive to both. The following guidelines will ensure that.

- Use white or off white paper printed on one side only.
- Provide a laser printed or first-run typed original if possible. Scanners need clear images.
- Do not fold, staple or attach paper clips.
- Use a standard 12-point font like Courier or Times New Roman.
- Do not use bolding, bullets, underlining, italics, special characters, dashes, images, graphics or borders.
- Place your name on its own line, at the top of each separate page.
- Employers frequently stipulate that covering letters and other attachments should not be sent at this stage.
- It is not as important to keep a scannable CV short. The software can easily handle multiple pages and will use all of the information it extracts to determine if your skills match available positions. Remember that it will also be read by a human at a later stage.

Keywords

Scanning software runs keyword searches on applications and selects on the basis of this. Keywords describe the skills required for each job, nouns as well as verbs. Scanning software may look for the names of programming languages and operating systems you are familiar with as well as words such as developed, initiated, managed. You can usually pick these words up from the job description. The words in bold in this advert would form the basis for your keyword response.

> We are looking for someone with a wide range of **teaching** and professional experience in **journalism**, ideally in both **print, broadcast** and **new media**. They will be required to **lead** a number of units that form part of the **practical work** on the **Media Studies** course. We welcome applications from those who can also teach **Web publishing** or contribute to the **theoretical units** on the **degree**. There is also an opportunity to develop your own **specialist area of teaching.** You will be expected to contribute to the **development** of the subject at **all levels**, and to the **administrative work** of the Media Studies Subject Group.

Each of the words highlighted is a general description of the skills needed for the job. It would be a mistake simply to repeat them in the application. Use of industry jargon is acceptable in these circumstances, it may form part of the keyword search. Keywords should elaborate and specify. Instead of saying you are proficient in the use of desktop publishing software, name the packages you have used. It is not enough to say you have extensive teaching, writing or broadcasting experience; name your specialist area, publications and programmes you have contributed to, list practical skills individually. The employer is using general terms in the advert to attract a wide range of applicants; you need to be more precise to attract him or her. Using keywords is equally valuable in applications that are not scanned electronically.

CVs that are e-mailed

Employers usually make it clear how they would like to receive e-mailed CVs. Some ask for certain file attachments, others prefer them as part of the body text of an e-mail. For information on sending attachments with e-mail, see page 157.

If you're going to send your CV as e-mail text you need to check it will work with most programs. Go for simplicity, even if you've got all sorts of clever formatting tools on your mail package. Assume the recipient can only cope with basic text. If you want to see what your CV looks like as an e-mail, put it in your outbox and look at it or send it to yourself (see Figure 5.8). However, your mail reading software may not be the same as the recipient's. The following guidelines will ensure that the appearance of a plain text CV will be acceptable on most browsers.

- Compose your CV in a word processing programme, spell check it, save as plain text, then copy and paste it into an e-mail. Check appearance and spacing, edit as necessary.

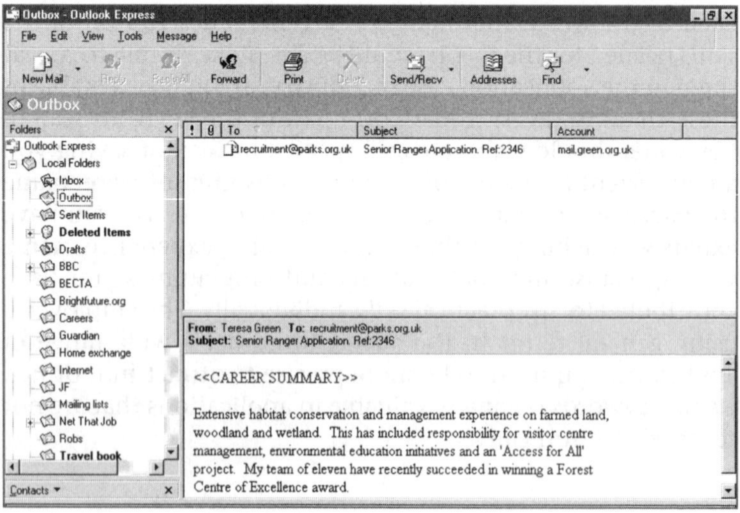

Figure 5.8 Looking at your CV in the outbox gives an idea of what your recipient will see

- Always complete the subject line. If it's in response to an advertised post, then 'Application for . . .' is sufficient. If it's a speculative application you have to be more imaginative in order to get the recipient to read it.
- Most screens show about twenty lines of text. Half of this may be taken up with the e-mail organization window. The first screen may only show a few lines of text. It should be interesting enough to encourage the recipient to go on to the next.
- The sender's name and e-mail always appear at the top of a message; don't fill the first screen with your contact details, put them at the end. Start with a career summary or employment objective instead.
- E-mail screens only allow 65–75 characters (including spaces) to a line. Use the word count facility on your word processing programs to check the number of characters.
- You cannot use formatting tools, but can highlight text by using characters such as – * = ~ ^ + < >.
- As with formatting on word processing programs, use it sparingly.

MATCHING APPLICATIONS TO VACANCIES

The need to tailor applications to specific vacancies is universally recognized. It is useful to place an employment objective, career or skill summary at the top of the page. This should relate to the job advertised and be in harmony with the aims and ethos of the employer you are contacting. Employee profiles, mission statements and job descriptions are a good way to research this. For general applications whether to an employer or an agency, there is still a need to include a career objective and/or skill summary.

Speculative applications

If your application will be held by a company for a period of time and matched against vacancies that arise, you need to be aware of the range of jobs they offer. Your application needs to be constructed in such a way that it will be considered for as many suitable vacancies as possible. Intel is one employer that uses this recruitment practice. Their site offers advice on how to prepare effective scannable CVs and includes examples that conform to their guidelines.

> Searches are done by keywords and phrases that describe the skills and core course work required for each job. It is important therefore that résumés include terms and familiar industry acronyms for all relevant skills and experience that could be of value in a position at Intel.
>
> A résumé should summarise skills in a clear and concise manner. Intel views a résumé as a demonstration of an applicant's ability to communicate. It should include all basic information: header, objective, education, key courses/skills, work experience, activities and interests. It should be customised to reflect specific career/job objectives. Recommended length is 1–2 pages. Cover letters should be brief and to the point; details should be included on the résumés.
>
> Intel Corporation

Bank CVs

If you are posting your CV on a database or registering it with an employment agency, you need to be clear in your own mind about the response you want to attract. If your CV is too general or too specific you may not get any offers at all. Most CV banks and agencies operate a system where the employer pays to access CV details. These agencies aim to make their database attractive to employers. This means having a good supply of well-qualified candidates from a range of occupational backgrounds. Consequently they offer help with the construction and presentation of applications to enable clients to contribute to their success.

Some agencies have relatively simple forms for you to complete online, with dropdown menus to aid selection of key skills and other criteria. Others have application forms as complex and detailed as any employer. They decide the format so every CV on their database has the same appearance; only the content differs. Wideyes incorporate sophisticated personality tests into the registration programme, making it easy for employers to select the best-matched candidates for their vacancies and company culture.

Figure 5.9 One CV can go a long way on the internet at `www.wideeyes.com`

INTERVIEWS

The final hurdle is the interview itself. This can range from an exchange of e-mails to a two-day ordeal including group discussion, tests, presentations and other exercises periodically favoured by recruiters. Preparation increases effectiveness and can help minimize stress and nervousness.

The employer is looking to choose the best person from a small number of applicants. Each of these has been judged to have the potential to be successful. The 'best' does not necessarily mean the most qualified. At this stage employers are looking at motivation, understanding of the company and the post plus compatibility with the existing team.

If you've got this far you will already have done most of the research you need. It is useful to look again at press releases and other information close to the interview date. Most company Web sites have this facility, even if they are not advertising jobs on their site. The latest issues of the related professional or trade journal are worth a revisit, and a quick search amongst online news archives like *The Times* (`www.the-times.co.uk`) or the BBC (`www.bbc.co.uk`) might help prevent you putting your foot in it. It should also help you answer questions, and ask some of your own, in a way that shows you are informed about the company and wider issues affecting your occupational area.

All the places that offer help with CVs give advice on interview technique and assessment centres. Careers advice, newspaper and recruitment Web sites are full of help to get you through the final stages of securing the job you want.

Finally you have to come out from behind your computer – e-mails are no substitute for eye contact. Equipped with the tools and knowledge from your electronic expeditions, you'll be in a strong position to secure work that suits you and develop a satisfying career. Once in a job, the Web still has its uses!

Figure 5.10 Perhaps Jo needs to start all over again. Follow her ups and downs at `www.revolver.com`

SITES WORTH SEEING

Many of the sites listed in earlier chapters offer help with applications and interview techniques. Most of the employment agencies listed in Chapter 4 have CV banks. Particularly useful sites for investigating application and interview techniques include:

Active Connection

`www.activeconnection.co.uk`

The 'Job Workout' section helps you tone up your CV and interview technique.

BBC Job Jungle

`www.bbc.co.uk/education/workskills/jobs/index.shtml`

Comprehensive guide to techniques for making effective applications.

Career Mosaic

`www.careermosaic-uk.co.uk`

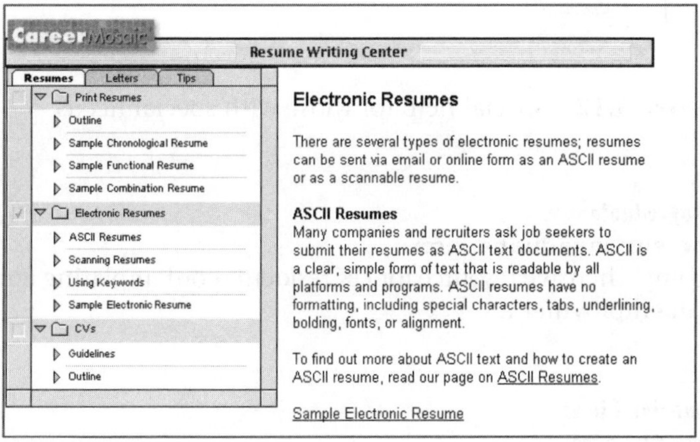

Figure 5.11 Visit the Resume Writing Centre for detailed information on writing every sort of application

Computer Weekly

`www.computerweekly.com`

The 'Job Advisor' section has help pages on CVs, interviews and freelance work.

Employability

`www.nrec.org.uk/employability`

Interactive package for disabled jobseekers with sections on how to tackle disability issues in applications and interviews.

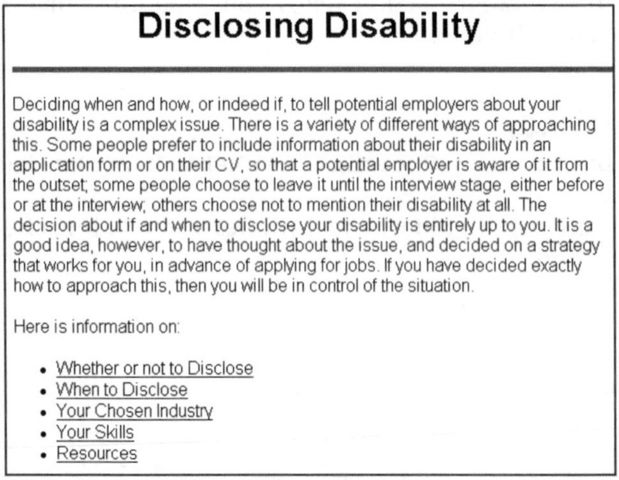

Disclosing Disability

Deciding when and how, or indeed if, to tell potential employers about your disability is a complex issue. There is a variety of different ways of approaching this. Some people prefer to include information about their disability in an application form or on their CV, so that a potential employer is aware of it from the outset; some people choose to leave it until the interview stage, either before or at the interview; others choose not to mention their disability at all. The decision about if and when to disclose your disability is entirely up to you. It is a good idea, however, to have thought about the issue, and decided on a strategy that works for you, in advance of applying for jobs. If you have decided exactly how to approach this, then you will be in control of the situation.

Here is information on:

- Whether or not to Disclose
- When to Disclose
- Your Chosen Industry
- Your Skills
- Resources

Figure 5.12 Special help for those with special needs

Eurograduate

`www.eurograduate.com`

A comprehensive resource for UK residents contemplating European employment.

Financial Times

`www.ft.com`

Detailed help with applications and interviews in the 'Careers Advisor' section.

GTI

www.gti.co.uk

The 'Dr. Job' section has excellent and amusing help with all aspects of application and interview. Laugh while you learn.

Gradunet

www.gradunet.co.uk/applications

Fill in a standard template with your common data, then whenever you apply online through Gradunet, your personal profile is automatically entered into the company's application form, allowing you to spend less time answering the laborious questions and more time on the important ones.

Monster

www.monster.co.uk

Help with applications, interviews and selection tests available from Monster's Career Centre.

Netwise

www.netwise.ac.uk

The pages of the careers service for the University of Manchester and UMIST have extensive information on applications, interviews, tests, assessment centres, employment law and equal opportunities.

Revolver

www.revolver.com

Vacancies from *The Times* and *Sunday Times* with information on CVs, letter writing and interview techniques.

Rise

www.jobsunlimited.co.uk/rise

Weekly supplement from *The Guardian* with articles to help you apply successfully for the jobs they advertise. Aimed at new graduates and professionals (see Figure 5.13).

Top Jobs

www.topjobs.co.uk

Employment agency that targets graduates and professionals. There is extensive help and advice on psychometric tests and the chance to complete online questionnaires to get you thinking about the things that really matter.

Total Jobs

www.totaljobs.com

The 'Careers Advisor' section offers information on coping with applications, interviews and selection tests.

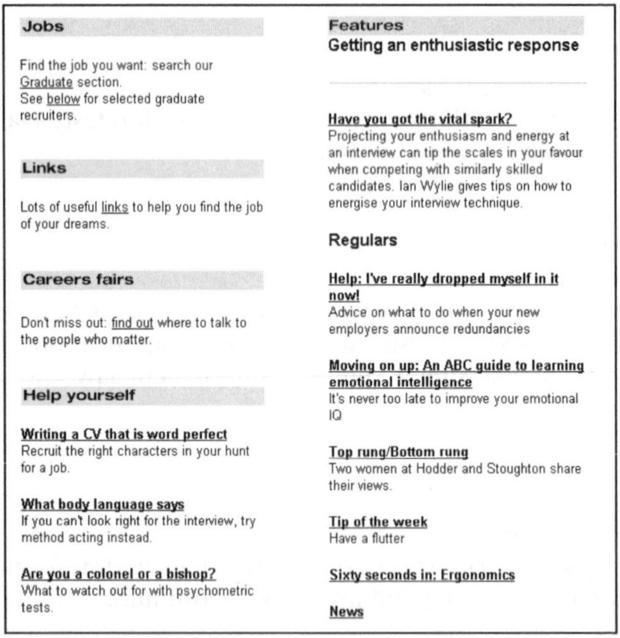

Jobs

Find the job you want: search our Graduate section.
See below for selected graduate recruiters.

Links

Lots of useful links to help you find the job of your dreams.

Careers fairs

Don't miss out: find out where to talk to the people who matter.

Help yourself

Writing a CV that is word perfect
Recruit the right characters in your hunt for a job.

What body language says
If you can't look right for the interview, try method acting instead.

Are you a colonel or a bishop?
What to watch out for with psychometric tests.

Features

Getting an enthusiastic response

Have you got the vital spark?
Projecting your enthusiasm and energy at an interview can tip the scales in your favour when competing with similarly skilled candidates. Ian Wylie gives tips on how to energise your interview technique.

Regulars

Help: I've really dropped myself in it now!
Advice on what to do when your new employers announce redundancies

Moving on up: An ABC guide to learning emotional intelligence
It's never too late to improve your emotional IQ

Top rung/Bottom rung
Two women at Hodder and Stoughton share their views.

Tip of the week
Have a flutter

Sixty seconds in: Ergonomics

News

Figure 5.13 Rise has advice to help you get a job and get on

WORTH REMEMBERING

- Writing your own CV is a valuable exercise. Excellent help with this can be found on the Web.
- Electronic application makes all forms look the same and removes many distractions for both writer and reader.
- Applications and CVs need to be constructed and presented in a way that takes account of how they will be sent and received.
- Employer Web sites are essential reading for effective interview preparation.
- Interview and assessment centre techniques can be learnt and practised using Web-based information.

APPENDIX 1 – MASTERING THE INTERNET

THE BASICS

Employers need workers who are computer literate. For many jobs it's as essential as conventional literacy. Skills you develop whilst using the internet to find work will help you whatever job you go for. It's one of the easiest technologies to master, but it can take a little practice to learn how to use your time effectively and find the information you want.

> This appendix is a guide to developing good browsing habits that minimize frustrations and save time and money.

There are lots of misconceptions about what the internet is, what it does, the benefits and dangers it brings.

WHAT'S NEEDED?

All you need is an interest in finding out more.
The internet:

- is a network of linked computers and other electronic devices such as mobile phones, televisions and even watches;
- is a way of moving information around the world quickly and efficiently;

- enables people to share information in a way that promotes understanding, allows free speech, encourages learning and the exchange of ideas;
- allows the unscrupulous to exploit others' vulnerabilities, invade privacy and defraud, but organizations and systems exist to help protect you from this.

Public internet access

You don't even have to own a computer – if you're uncertain whether the internet has anything to offer you, try it first using public access. It's a cheap way to find out more and often comes with help and technical support thrown in. Places offering public access include:

Libraries

Many offer internet access and short courses to get you started. They normally charge around £5 an hour.

Job Centres

Offer free internet access to help jobseekers find work.

Cybercafes

Are places where you can eat, drink and access the internet. You'll find them in Yellow Pages, usually listed under computer services. Once you're on the internet you can find cybercafes in all parts of the world from `www.netcafeguide.com`

Schools and colleges

Many offer introductory internet courses and use of their computers. This is normally outside normal teaching hours and can be linked to training and childcare. Contact Learn Direct for details of courses in your area on 0800 100 900.

National events

The BBC runs an annual campaign called Computers Don't Bite. This includes TV programmes and free 'taster sessions' in libraries, shopping centres, buses and pubs. An initiative called IT FOR ALL offers a free, easy-to-read guide on all aspects of information technology, details of courses and computer access points in your locality. Contact them on 0800 456 567.

Friends and relatives

People with internet access are often happy to share their discoveries with you, particularly if you cover the phone costs for time you spend online.

Internet through your TV

A growing number of services offer internet access through your TV – in some cases through a video game console. At the moment this is more limited and less flexible than using a computer, but it's an area that's changing quickly. A typical package includes a charge for installation and a monthly charge – usually subject to taking out a 12-month contract. Some services offer access to the whole internet, others to pre-selected sites only. Most connect via your phone line so incur the usual call charges.

Examples of current providers include NTL, who offer access to the whole internet via TV and your phone line. Cable and Wireless offer access to pre-selected sites via cable TV which means your phone line is not tied up and there are no call charges. If you're a Sky subscriber, investigate Open. SEGA's Dreamcast games console incorporates TV internet via your phone, and more games companies are planning to enter this market.

Mobile phone access to the Internet

Hailed as the future, hand-held devices offer a new way of accessing some internet information. Still in the early stages of development, it's moving quickly and employment agencies such as Gis-a-Job (`www.gisajob.com`) make their site available through WAP enabled phones. At the moment, information is only from a few providers on selected topics such as news updates, sports headlines, weather, travel information and last-minute holiday offers, but it looks set to grow. There's also an increasing convergence between e-mail and mobile phone messaging (see page 168).

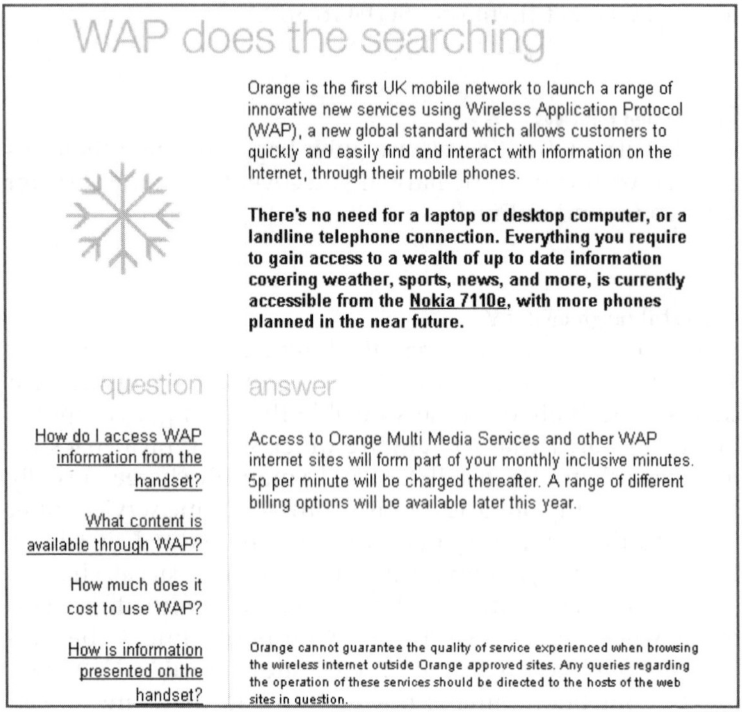

WAP does the searching

Orange is the first UK mobile network to launch a range of innovative new services using Wireless Application Protocol (WAP), a new global standard which allows customers to quickly and easily find and interact with information on the Internet, through their mobile phones.

There's no need for a laptop or desktop computer, or a landline telephone connection. Everything you require to gain access to a wealth of up to date information covering weather, sports, news, and more, is currently accessible from the Nokia 7110e, with more phones planned in the near future.

question	answer
How do I access WAP information from the handset?	Access to Orange Multi Media Services and other WAP internet sites will form part of your monthly inclusive minutes. 5p per minute will be charged thereafter. A range of different billing options will be available later this year.
What content is available through WAP?	
How much does it cost to use WAP?	
How is information presented on the handset?	Orange cannot guarantee the quality of service experienced when browsing the wireless internet outside Orange approved sites. Any queries regarding the operation of these services should be directed to the hosts of the web sites in question.

Figure A1.1 The future of internet access? BT Cellnet and Vodafone have WAP services too

The main difference between these ways of accessing the net is:

- A computer has a memory and therefore the facility to store material. This means you can read previously visited Web pages offline, compose or read e-mail offline and save Web and e-mail files.
- A TV-based system does not have a memory so everything you do that needs internet access has to be done online which can lead to high call costs.
- Mobile phones have some memory. Internet access via mobiles is limited at the moment but it is growing fast.

Doing it with a computer

Computers remain the most popular way of accessing the internet. If you decide to go for personal access through your computer, you will also need a modem, browser software and a phone. Most computers bought in the last few years will be internet ready. If your computer doesn't have a modem you can buy one for less than £50. If you are using an older computer check whether its speed and memory will be able to cope with the demands you'll be putting on it. The companies that provide the service that connects you to the internet (Internet Service Providers) generally recommend a minimum of 16 MB of RAM and 80 MB of hard disk space.

A modem allows your computers to communicate with other computers through the phone system. The faster your modem and computer, the quicker you receive and send information. This minimizes time spent connected to the phone (online), which usually has a cost attached to it. A modem can also act as an answering and fax machine when linked to your computer. This is independent of the internet and a valuable extra resource, so check for these facilities.

Your modem connects into your phone line. The easiest way is to get a 'doubler' for your phone. You then plug your modem and phone into the same line. Because the line is shared, you will not be able to use both at the same time. To use both together, you'll have to install an extra line.

You'll also need software called a Web browser. The most commonly used is Microsoft's Internet Explorer. It's a free product and may already be on your computer. If not, you should be able to get one as part of a free start up package from any Internet Service Provider (ISP). You need an account with an ISP to connect to the internet. Some organizations charge a monthly fee, but a growing number offer such services for free.

CHOOSING AN INTERNET SERVICE PROVIDER

Internet Service Providers are commercial organizations that link you to the rest of the world through their computers. When you connect to the internet your first call is to your ISP and should only be a local call.

Most internet users no longer pay a subscription to their ISP.

There are over 400 free providers in the UK; many offer incentives to persuade you to use their service rather than that of their competitors. One of the largest is Freeserve (**`www.freeserve.net`**) from the Dixons Group. This is a full internet access service with no registration or subscription fees and no hourly online charges. It gives unlimited access to the internet, newsgroups, unlimited e-mail addresses as well as space to create your own Web site. Other free providers include Tesco (**`www.tesco.net`**), Arsenal Football Club (**`www.arsenal.co.uk`**), Virgin Net (**`www.virgin.net`**), the BBC (**`www.freebeeb.net`**), and LineOne (**`www.lineone.net`**). Installation software can be ordered from their Web sites or picked up from retail stores they have a connection with.

Look out for reduced rate or free internet call offers from ISPs. This is becoming a common feature. There's a strong possibility that call costs will continue to drop or perhaps disappear altogether in the future. In the meantime it pays to shop around and compare. An excellent starting point for this is Net4Nowt; their site includes a list of ISPs and they keep you updated on latest offers and associated problems.

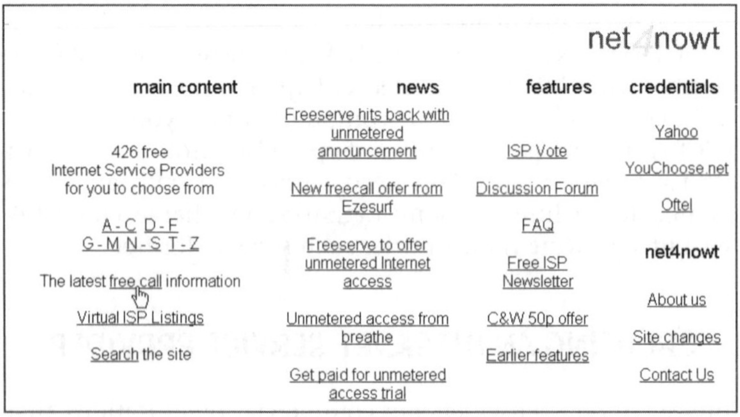

Figure A1.2 Confused by all the different free offers? **`www.net4nowt.com`** compares them for you

Some free deals are dependent on spending a certain amount on national and international calls or on buying a certain number of shares in the company, subject to an initial sign-up fee or monthly subscription charge. Before switching to a new and unknown provider, try them alongside your existing one. Services with free phone numbers can be permanently engaged or painfully slow. One of the most reliable sources of information on how good unmetered ISPs are is the comments section of Net4Nowt's pages on free call providers. Performance is not constant and can deteriorate suddenly if providers take on more users than they can cope with.

Other points to check

The cost of calls to help lines

Free providers can charge up to £1 a minute. However, many have extensive online help and offer additional support through e-mail and newsgroups so you can sort out problems easily once you're online.

Software compatibility

Some providers may use software that requires the latest operating system or is not compatible with yours. If you need to buy a new computer to make use of a free service then it might not be quite the bargain it first appears.

E-mail

Some providers only offer Web-based e-mail, which means you have to be online to compose and read mail. It's better to get a POP 3 mail account (see page 155); many free services include this.

Availability of online or e-mail help

This is particularly important if their help line is expensive to access.

You'll be able to get answers to these questions from the company's customer service department, the store you get your free software from or their Web site.

KEEPING SAFE

Information on the internet can come from any individual or organization. There is no real control and little censorship. This has led to many well-publicized horror stories, and indeed there is much that is truly horrible. Internet software allows you to regulate what is accessed. The most basic form of control is contained in the browser software, such as the **Content Advisor** on Microsoft Internet Explorer. There's a range of additional, more sophisticated filtering software available from sites listed at the end of this section. These are maintained by organizations working to make the internet a safe and positive experience for all.

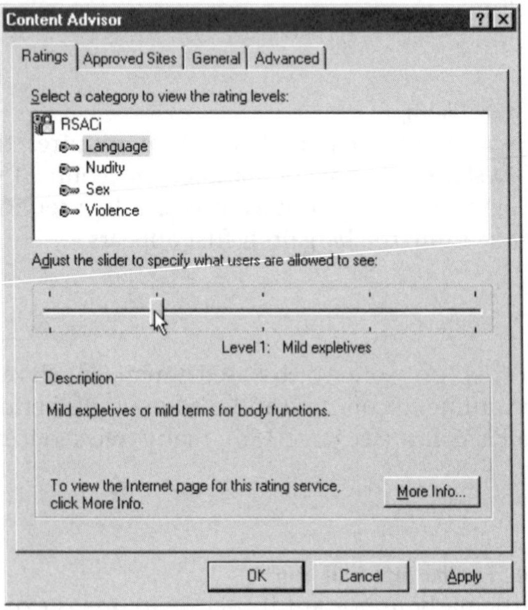

Figure A1.3 You can restrict the sites that can be accessed

Worries about the internet should not prevent you from looking at what it has to offer for you. That which is good far exceeds that which is not. This book points out worthwhile sites and helps you develop the techniques to find your own.

Personal safety

The internet is both personal and anonymous. People can hide their identity behind an e-mail address, and so can you. There is no problem until you start to divulge personal details. Take the usual precautions you would when dealing with any stranger. Because you can't see or hear the person it would be easy for someone to misrepresent him or herself. A '14-year-old girl' could in reality be a 50-year-old man. If you are aware of the dangers, you can make internet use safer. If you come across something that offends you, close it down. You don't have to read or look at it.

Financial safety

Anyone can set up a Web site and claim to be whatever takes their fancy. Some sites belong to commercial companies, some to individuals or educational institutions who want to share rather than sell their knowledge. There are dishonest and dubious operations and individuals amongst them. It's up to you to look at the information with a critical eye, check that the companies you are dealing with are legitimate and that any money you part with is safe. Don't be taken in by the appearance of the site; a good-looking site is no guarantee of quality information or product. Many of the best sites have relatively plain interfaces.

Buying from the Web

Financial transactions on the Web should only be carried out on secure sites. Web browsers such as Internet Explorer use SSL (Secure Sockets Layer) that encrypts data you send so that no one can read or change it during transmission.

Secure sites have a URL or Web site address that starts with https and a closed padlock in the bottom right-hand section of your browser.

You can send your credit card number to a secure site as safely as giving your details over the phone. It doesn't remove all the risks. You are trusting the server administrator with your credit card number and no technology can protect you from dishonest or careless people.

Commercial fraud that existed before the internet exists on it. New technologies enable new ways of perpetrating fraud but also provide new methods of combating it. There is excellent guidance to this on the Department of Trade and Industry's Consumer Affairs Web site, `www.consumer.gov.uk`

Computer safety

A computer virus is a piece of code designed to disrupt the operation of a computer. Files containing viruses can be transmitted across the internet through file downloads or e-mail attachments. Your browser will normally display a warning when you're about to download or open the type of file that could contain a virus. To protect yourself, only download files from sources you know are safe.

> Make sure you have up-to-date virus software correctly installed before downloading anything from the Web.

Viruses are usually hidden in programs and activated when the programs run. It's essential to install software that checks for this before you download anything from the Web or open an e-mail attachment. If you have a virus it can sometimes be 'cleaned up' by this software. To get full protection make sure you run the program as recommended and update it regularly.

Documents attached to e-mails can carry a virus if they contain a macro. You will normally receive a warning if you try to open an attachment that could contain harmful files.

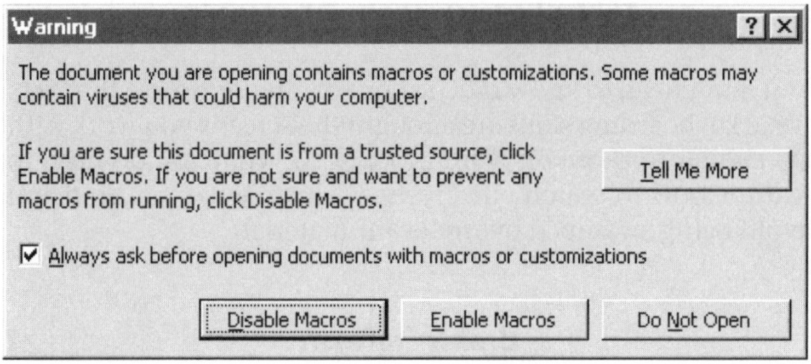

Figure A1.4 Be careful about what you open or download

Evaluating information

Worthwhile sites usually state their purpose clearly and explain who they are in an 'About Us' section. Be sceptical of sites where you can't find answers to the following:

- Who owns the site?
- What's their main purpose – selling, educating or entertaining?
- Would you trust this company/individual/organization to provide accurate, reliable information in real life?
- When was the information last updated?
- Is there real-world contact information?

> Anything that sounds too good to be true probably is. Many 'make money from home' scams have been adapted to 'make money from the internet' and are best avoided.

Very little information is truly objective. Reputable sources such as universities, government departments, newspapers, broadcasters, learned societies and publishers have sites with information which is comprehensive, accurate and up to date, but they all have a point of view to promote.

MASTERING YOUR BROWSER

You don't need to know much about computers to use the Web. Basic keyboarding skills are enough; the screens you work with are similar to those on word processors. What you do need to learn is how to search effectively, evaluate what you find and avoid being swamped by irrelevant material.

Browser software

You look at and move around Web pages using a browser. Internet Explorer 5 (IE5) is used in the screen shots in this book, but its appearance and functions are similar to other browsers. Like everything else associated with the internet, browsers are continually being upgraded. If you want to keep up with developments, look at **www.browsers.com**

> It's not necessary to have the most up to date browser. In some cases an older computer may not be powerful enough to run the latest browser software.

You can look at browser software and previously visited Web pages without being connected to the phone. Spending time offline getting used to the layout and functions of your browser costs nothing. Then when you go online, you will be familiar with the commands and able to work quickly.

A Web page may take up more space than your screen can display. Use the scroll bar or page down key to move through it.

Your pointer is used to move around the screen. When it meets a link it changes from an arrow to a hand with a pointing finger. Links to other pages or sites can be coloured or underlined text or a picture. Clicking on a link takes you to the new page. Text links usually change colour to show they have been visited.

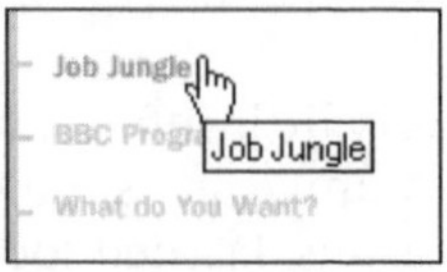

The status bar at the bottom of the

Web page lets you know what's going on. If you hover over a link, a summary of its content or an address will appear in the

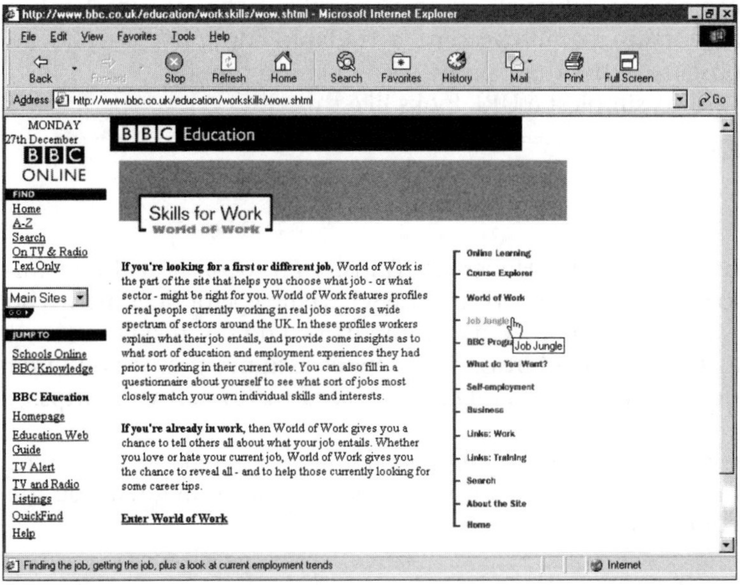

Figure A1.5 A typical browser page

status bar, to show where clicking on that link would take you. In this case it's another page on the same site, but it could be to another site anywhere in the world.

The Address Bar shows the address or URL of the Web page you are viewing.

To get started on the Web all you need to know is the address of the site you want to visit and where to type it in.

UNDERSTANDING WEB ADDRESSES

Every Web page has a unique address known as its Uniform Resource Locator or URL. These are a cross between a phone number and an address. You need the same complete accuracy when using it – one character wrong and you end up somewhere else, or nowhere at all. Like addresses, URLs contain information about their destination. If you understand what makes up an internet address you can try to put it right if it doesn't work. It can give you clues about who's providing the information but as domain names become a tradable commodity they can obscure rather than clarify who's behind the site.

At its simplest a URL looks like this.

What it all means

http: stands for Hypertext Transfer Protocol. It is always followed by //. It tells your browser what type of document you want. For normal Web documents you do not need to enter it as part of the address, the browser assumes that if you enter nothing, http:// should be there. Secure sites start with https://.

`www.bbc` is known as the domain name and tells you the name of the server and company/organization/individual you are connecting to.

.co. tells you what sort of organization it is. Commonly used ones are:

.ac	=	academic institution in the UK only. Elsewhere edu. is used;
.com	=	commercial company elsewhere and increasingly in the UK;
.gov	=	governmental organization;
.org	=	other types of organization;
.sch	=	school site;
.net	=	Internet Service Provider.

.uk This tells you in which country the site originates. Every country has its own code, eg fr = France; is = Iceland; ie = Ireland; za = South Africa; pl = Poland. USA Web sites do not normally use a country code.

> Resist the temptation to put a full stop at the end of a URL, there never is one!

The basic URL will generally take you to the Home Page of a Web site. This provides content lists or site maps to help you find your way around the site.

Finding specific files

URLs that extend beyond the country code are the addresses of specific pages or files. They are separated from the main body of the URL by a / (forward slash), eg **www.bbc.co.uk/education/workskills/wow/estate.shtml** is a page on BBC Education's 'Worlds of Work' site that contains a profile of an estate agent.

Specific files like these can change. If a URL is taking you to a current piece of information, that file may disappear when information is updated and trying to reach it will produce an error message. If this happens, go to the address bar and delete back as far as the first forward slash. Here that would be to **www.bbc.co.uk** (the site's home page). You can then use search or browse facilities to find the page you need.

If the site has moved there may be a message or link that will take you to the new address. If not you should be able to find a site's new location by searching for the site's name or the topic it deals with using one of the search tools described at the end of this section.

Using browser commands

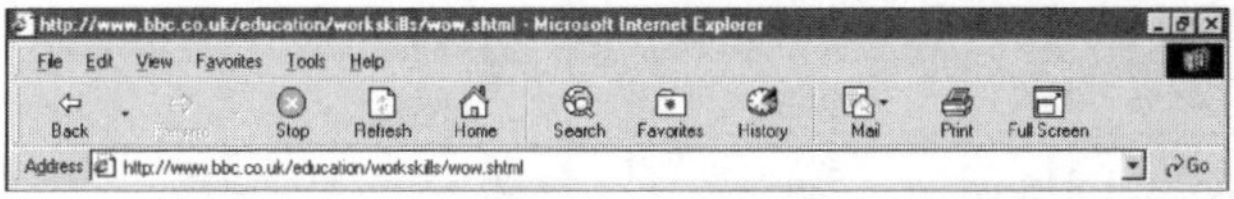

The commands for your browser are at the top of your screen. Each page starts with a title bar showing the name of the Web page. Below that is the menu bar, then the toolbar and address bar.

Commands from the menu bar enable you to carry out a range of functions. Experiment with these by working offline on any previously viewed page. Some to try include:

File/Save As . . .

Allows you to save a page and is one way of later using that information offline. IE 5 offers a **Save Web page complete** option. In earlier browsers this command saves only the text; pictures need to be saved separately.

File/Work Offline

Allows you to look at previously visited pages without connecting to the phone. For a more detailed explanation see page 147.

Favorites

When you are looking at a Web page you can add it to your **Favorites**. This means storing the address so you can return to it with a single click. To add a page to **Favorites** you select the **Add to Favorites** option. It's a good idea to make folders for different subjects so you can organize your bookmarks and make them easier to use. To add, remove or rename folders choose the **Organize Favorites** option.

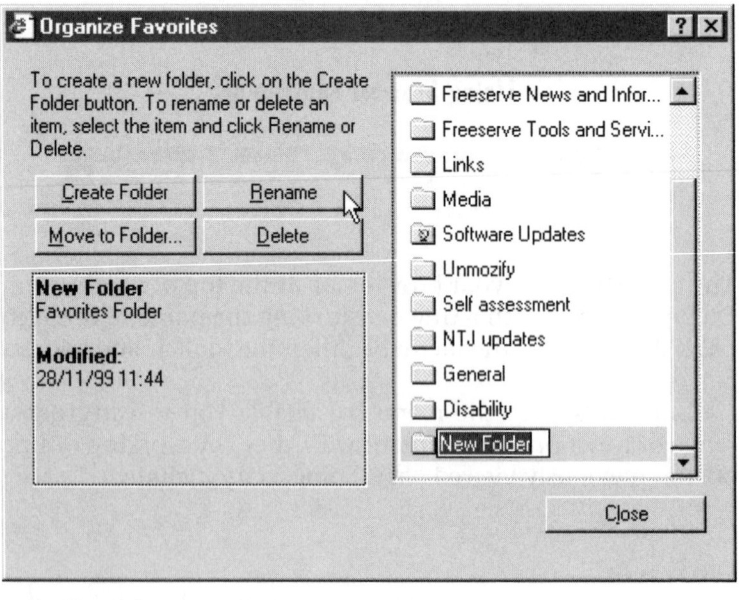

Figure A1.6 Well-organized Favorites make life a lot easier

Tools/internet options

This is where you go to control the way your Web pages look, the way the internet is accessed and to clean up temporary internet files. Basic changes to make Web pages more accessible to users with special needs can be accessed here (see Figure A1.7).

One setting worth changing is your choice of home page. It will have been set to connect you to the Web site of your ISP. You may prefer to start elsewhere. You can type in any address you want, choose the page you're currently viewing or use a blank page. If you always prefer to start by working offline, the simplest way is to set your home page as a blank. The command for this is on the **General** tab of **Internet options**.

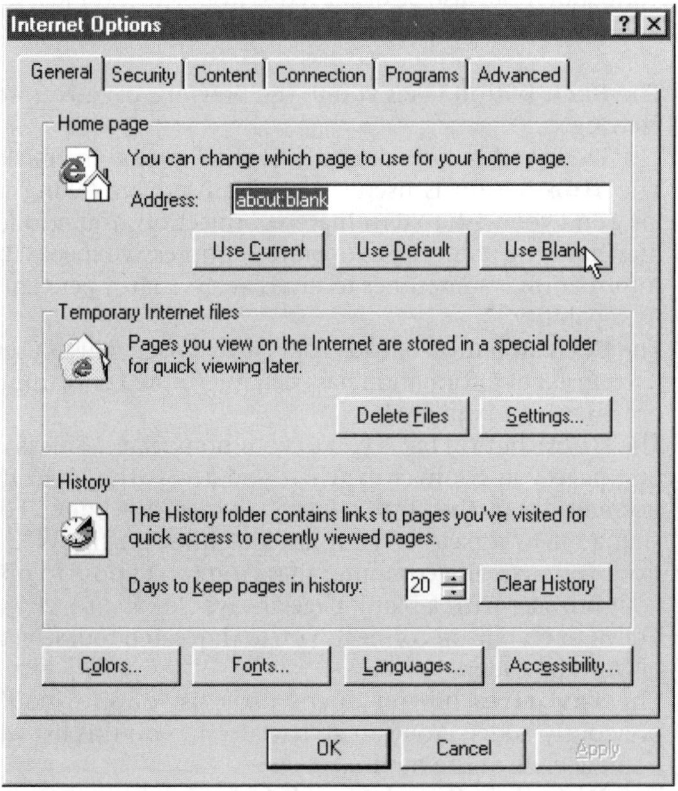

Figure A1.7 With a blank home page your browser doesn't try to dial up every time you open it

Help pages

All the software has help sections. You can print the pages that deal with relevant topics and explore your browser's operations without being online.

The toolbar

This has the popular commands from the menu bar. They are activated by a single click of the mouse. When not available to you the icons are 'greyed out'. Here the toolbar is in picture and text form, but it can also be displayed as just pictures or just text. It can be customized to show more or fewer buttons:

- The **Back** button takes you to the previous page you were viewing.
- The **Forward** button can only be used after going back.
- The **Stop** button is useful when transfers are taking too long and you wish to terminate a connection. Your modem may have the potential to operate at impressive speeds, but information is sometimes received at less than 1 per cent of its capability.
- The **Refresh** button reloads your current page. This is useful if a transfer of information has been interrupted or corrupted or you want to update it.
- The **Home** button takes you to your home page. This is the first page you connect to when you access the Web. It is normally set by the ISP to take you to their site, but you can change it to a page of your choice either on the Web or from your existing computer files. You can choose to open your browser with a blank page always (see Figure A1.7).
- The **Search** button connects you to the search tool selected by your provider.
- The **Favorites** button opens up a list of sites you've previously added. You can go back to sites on this list with a single click of the mouse.
- The **History** button shows a list of recently visited sites. You can use it for offline browsing.

- The **Mail** button opens your e-mail programme.
- The **Print** button prints the current Web page. A Web page can be several screen or paper pages long. To print specific pages use **File/Print** from the menu bar. Newer browsers have a print preview facility.
- The **Fullscreen** button allows the Web page to take up all of the screen.

To change which buttons are displayed on your toolbar, click the right button of your mouse anywhere in the toolbar and explore the **Customize** option.

WORKING OFFLINE

The pages of visited sites are stored as temporary internet files. You can look at most of them again without being connected to the phone, using the browser's **History** function and choosing the option to **Work Offline**. However, selecting **File/Work Offline** when you are connected to the internet does not disconnect you from the phone. It simply allows you to look at temporary internet files without trying to connect. Disconnect in the normal way first or open your browser as a blank page and select **Work Offline**.

The title bar tells you when you are working offline and a modem with cross symbol appears in the status bar.

Click on the **History** button to see a list of previously visited sites. With newer browsers you can search cached pages for a matching word or choose the order in which they are displayed (see Figure A1.8).

Not all pages in your history can be viewed offline. If your pointer changes to a hand with a no entry sign that link cannot be viewed offline. The same symbol appears if you try to follow a link you did not previously make. Clicking on an unavailable link will bring up a dialogue box that gives you the option to reconnect to the internet.

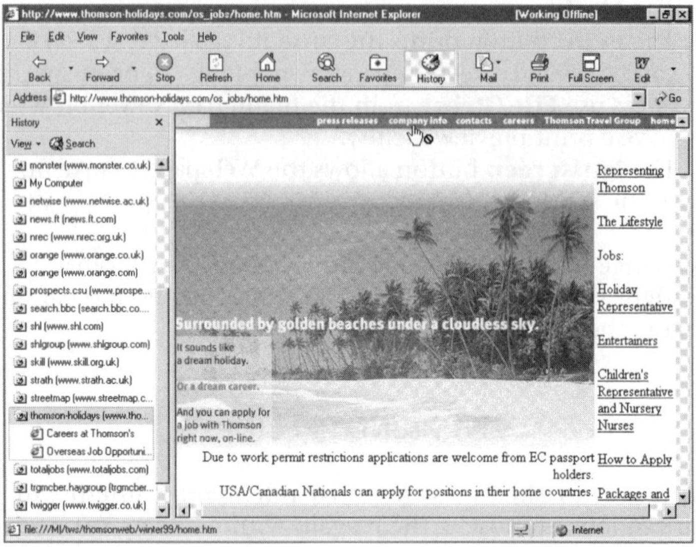

Figure A1.8 Most pages you access can be looked at again offline using the History button

DOWNLOADING DOCUMENTS AND PROGRAMS

As well as providing information, many sites give the option of downloading files. These can be documents, pictures, sound files, videos or programs. Once downloaded, that file is stored on your computer. Programs available may be freeware or shareware. Freeware is completely free; shareware normally gives you a free evaluation period after which you need to pay to continue to use the program.

If you're downloading a file you need to check that you have the software to open it. Common formats include document files (DOC) for Microsoft Word, and Portable Document Format (PDF) that requires Adobe Acrobat Reader. Many sites offer information in PDF format. If your computer does not have Adobe Acrobat it can be downloaded for free from **www.adobe.com** (see Figure A1.9).

Files can be compressed or zipped, which makes transmission faster. The standard program for dealing with these zip files is WinZip, available from **www.winzip.com/download/htm**

Cumbria County Council
E-mail
Information about Jobs in Cumbria
Cumbria County Council Jobs - 03/12
Cumbria County Council Jobs - 26/11
Other Jobs - 03/12
Other Jobs - 26/11
The Jobs Bulletins are in Adobe Acrobat (PDF) format. If you do not have the free Acrobat Reader (V3 or later) installed on your PC, you can download a copy by clicking on the icon below.
Get Acrobat Reader
Adobe

Figure A1.9 Sites that offer PDF documents usually provide a link to downloading the program needed to open them

To download a file all you need do is decide which directory you want to save it in. A dialogue box appears as you're downloading and shows progress (see Figure A1.10).

Plug-ins

A plug-in is a mini-program that adds extra functions. Some of the clever tricks Web sites perform need plug-ins like Shockwave or Real Audio to work (see Figure A1.11). Some sites won't work without plug-ins but the sensible ones are constructed with an option for plain versions, as some older computers and browsers won't cope with plug-ins. Sites that require additional software usually offer an option to download it for free.

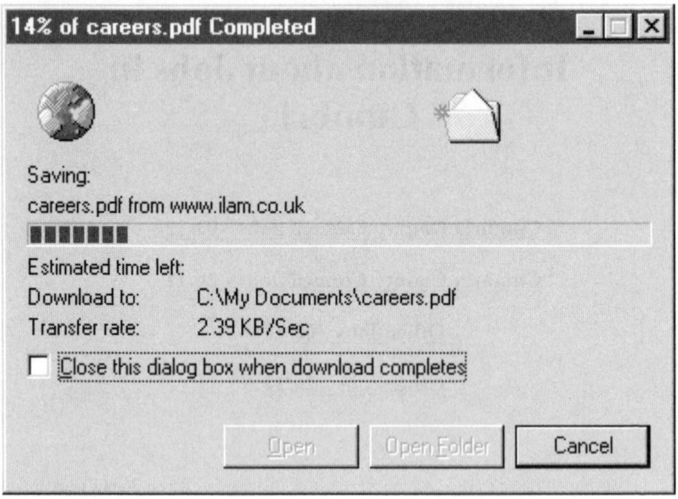

Figure A1.10 If it's taking too long to download, try at a less busy time

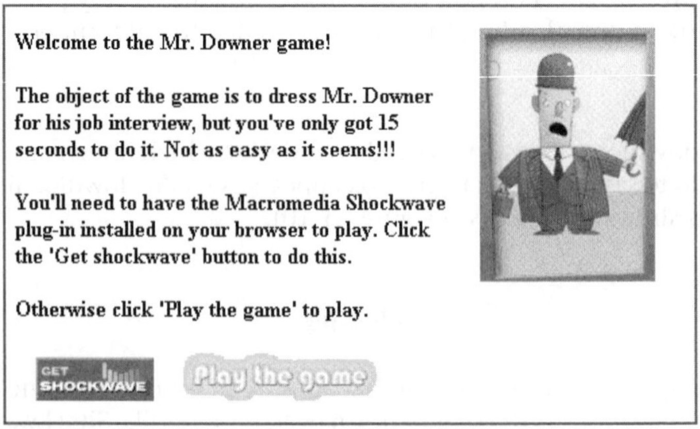

Figure A1.11 Plug-ins can bring your browser to life

Appendix 1

EFFECTIVE SEARCHING

Unlike other libraries of information there is no single classification system on the Web. It would be impossible to make use of this huge body of information without some index. Search engines, directories and Meta searchers act as index and contents pages for Web information. They are powerful tools that can help you find what you want. Many have enthusiastic sounding names like Yahoo!, Yell and Excite; they do behave in an enthusiastic manner, quickly fetching lots of interesting things for you to look at – which can cause problems. You get hundreds, thousands, even millions of documents if your search is too general and none if it's too specific.

Search tools

Your search button links to some search tools but you don't have to use just these. They have been selected by your provider for commercial reasons and may not be the best for your searches. Different directories and search engines are good for different things. Try the same query with a few to see which gives the best results.

Directories are compiled by humans with sites being assigned to appropriate sections. This means you can browse by category as well as entering key words for a search. Although this cuts down on irrelevant matches, directories can be small and give less comprehensive results than search engines. These run automatically, visiting a huge number of Web sites and newsgroups, constantly updating their content. They search on word match rather than context, which can result in a lot of irrelevant documents.

A good way to find which search tool is producing the best results is to use a Meta search like Dogpile, **www.dogpile.com** This sends your query to 24 searchers at once, then displays results for each. It's not unusual to have one search engine returning no matches whilst another finds hundreds. Dogpile is a quick way to discover which are likely to deal best with your particular query.

Careers and job vacancy sites abound on the Web. You are likely to be swamped rather than experience a shortage of places to visit. Choose any search tool from those described at the end of this chapter to start with, but don't restrict yourself to one searcher – they all find different things.

Language is full of ambiguities that are not always understood by computer searches. As well as using the right search tool you've got to think of how to put keywords together to help them recognize what you're really looking for.

If you enter the words 'Manchester Careers' in a search tool like Alta Vista it will produce over 4 million matches. It finds all the pages containing the words 'Manchester' and all the pages containing the word 'careers' and any pages that contain the phrase 'Manchester Careers'. If you refine that search so it sees the words as a phrase, the result is 40 Web pages, all of which refer to organizations providing careers advice in Manchester.

Most search tools allow you to narrow your search and include or exclude things with, for example, the simple option of matching any or all of your words. Details are in their help sections.

If you're getting too many or too few matches, take time to look at these help sections. One common system for refining searches is shown below.

Simple keyword search query:
Manchester:
This query will return all sites containing the word Manchester

Boolean query:
Manchester AND Careers / Manchester + Careers
This query will return all sites that contain both words anywhere in the object in any order

Negated query:
Manchester AND NOT Careers / Manchester - Careers
This query will return all sites that contain the word Manchester and don't contain the word Careers

Phrase query:
"Manchester Careers"
This query will return all sites that contain Manchester Careers as a phrase

Figure A1.12 How you phrase your search makes a difference

Most search engines offer the choice between concentrating on an individual country or searching worldwide. Yahoo!, for example, has specific search engines for most countries in the world.

Another effective way of finding worthwhile sites is to use a 'Web Guide'. These differ from search tools in that they make judgements on the quality of a site's information and provide a review of it. BBC Education's 'Web Guide', for example, at **www.bbc.co.uk/education/webguide** has a regularly updated careers advice section (see Figure 3.9). There is a more general, adult oriented guide to the best of the Web at: **www.bbc.co.uk/webguide**

ACCESSIBILITY FOR DISABLED USERS

For those with disabilities, the easy communication made possible by the internet holds the promise of removing many barriers. Much thought and effort have been put into making the internet accessible to all users.

Web designers are being encouraged to develop pages with accessibility in mind, taking into consideration the needs of those with limited dexterity, visually impairment and dyslexia. The Centre for Applied Special Technology (CAST) provides a service that analyses Web page accessibility. Pages that meet their standards can display the 'Bobby' symbol.

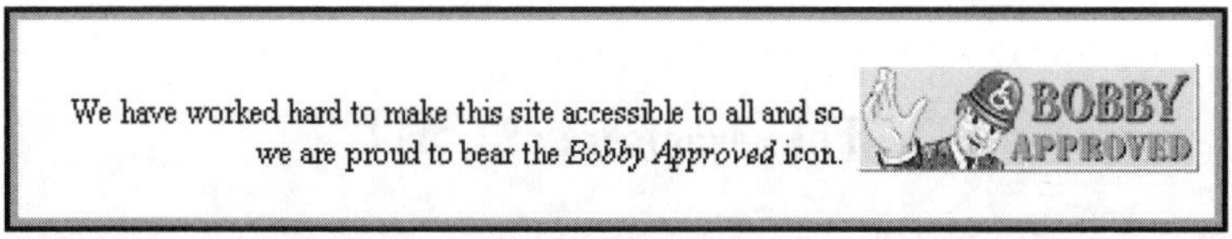

We have worked hard to make this site accessible to all and so we are proud to bear the *Bobby Approved* icon.
BOBBY
APPROVED

Figure A1.13 Bobby approved pages meet the browsing needs of those with disabilities

The BBC has developed software called BETSIE (BBC Education Text to Speech Internet Enhancer). This runs on their own and many other sites to help alleviate some of the problems experienced by blind people using screen readers for browsing. Screen readers enable computers to read computer pages to those who can't see them. BETSIE pages are plain text and can be easier to read than colourful, image-rich pages. Find out more at `www.bbc.co.uk/education/betsie`.

Customizing page appearance

If the way a Web page is presented makes it difficult for you to use, most browsers will allow you to alter its appearance. Details vary between browsers, but can always be found in the **Help** section. In IE5, basic changes can be made by selecting the **Accessibility** option from the **General** tab in the **internet Options** dialogue box (see Figure A1.7).

On Microsoft Windows 95 and later versions there is an accessibility option in the **Control Panel**. It allows you to select settings that apply to all programs and enables you to customize page appearance and keyboard use.

GETTING THE MOST FROM E-MAIL

E-mail is the most widely used tool on the internet. It's a cheap and efficient way of communicating. When you set up an internet account you will normally get at least one mailbox and e-mail address. Once you have access to the Web you'll find all sorts of organizations offering free e-mail accounts.

The advantages of e-mail

- You can send messages, attach pictures, documents, programs, videos or sound files to anyone else who has an e-mail address.
- It is easy to send copies of the same message to different people.
- There is no need to worry about time zones, an e-mail sent in the middle of the night doesn't wake anyone.
- Messages and attachments can be printed or stored on a computer.

- It costs the same to send whatever the destination.
- Where an e-mail can't be delivered it is generally returned to the sender with an explanation of the problem.

The disadvantages of e-mail

- You have to pay to look at your e-mail because you go online to receive it.
- E-mail is not always totally reliable. Mail can disappear completely, pretty much like conventional mail, although this only happens rarely.
- Text messages transfer quickly but graphics and attachments can take a long time. You can instruct your browser not to accept e-mails above a certain size.
- Computer viruses can be spread by e-mail.

Free accounts

If you don't have an internet account, or frequently change providers, it's easy to get a free account. You can have a:

- POP 3 account that uses your existing mail software.
- Web-based mail that is accessed through a Web site and does not need mail software.
- Forwarding account that sends your e-mail to any other account you choose.

You can of course have all of these plus your regular ISP account and use each for different purposes.

POP3 mail

POP stands for Post Office Protocol and is the way your software communicates with mail servers. To read this type of mail you need a standard internet POP-client, such as Outlook Express, Eudora, Pegasus Mail or Netscape Mail. You normally get this type of account from your ISP.

Incoming messages are stored on a server and remain there until you connect and download the messages to your computer. The big advantage of this is that you can write and read messages offline and use your software package to organize your mail.

Web-based e-mail

With these services you log into a Web site to access your e-mail. This means that mail has to be composed, read and organized whilst you are online. Messages can be printed, saved, copied and pasted to a word processing application. Different Web-based free e-mail services come with different tools, such as spell checkers, address books and folder systems. There are hundreds of such services; one of the best known is Hotmail (`www.hotmail.com`). To find others, take a look at `www.emailaddresses.com` (see Figure A1.17).

Email and mobile phones

It's possible to send an e-mail that appears as a text message on any mobile phone. There are restrictions to the length of messages but the free services offered are worth investigating. As well as a range of messaging options there are diary facilities on sites like BT Cellnet's Genie: `www.genie.co.uk`

Forwarding services

Some providers of free e-mail addresses act as forwarders as well. This means they automatically send on mail from your free address to any e-mail address you nominate. The result is that you can have one e-mail address that will not change regardless of how many times you change provider. You can alter where mail is forwarded to easily or choose to leave it in a Web-based post box.

The domain names offered by free services are often much more individual than those you get from your ISP. You can set up different ones for different purposes, depending on the impression you want to create like:

- never@atwork.com
- busy@alltimes.com

Is there a catch?

Not really. They collect any personal information you choose to give them and may sell this on to advertisers. Some forwarding services may make their more attractive addresses free for a limited period only; others are free forever. Some companies and ISPs may block e-mails from certain free addresses because of worries that junk mailers and crooks hide behind the anonymity such addresses offer.

POP3 gateway services

A number of sites, for example **www.twigger.co.uk** and also **www.icmessaging.co.uk** let you access your POP3 account from any computer. You need to know your login name, password and in some cases your mail server address. Details will be shown on your dial up connection, otherwise ask your provider.

Understanding e-mail addresses

Typical addresses will look like:

- me@free-mail.com
- irene@companyname.freecalls.co.uk
- rds@jobs4u.co.uk

They are similar to URLs and require the same attention to accuracy. The first part of the address is the name you choose for yourself. It may not always be your first name or initials because once a name has been allocated, it cannot be used by anyone else. If the name you want has been taken you have to use a certain amount of ingenuity in choosing one to represent you. Your name or number is always followed by @ which means at. The next part shows whom your account is with and follows the same conventions as URLs.

E-mail attachments

Any file on your computer can be sent with your e-mail (see Figure A1.14). All mail programs have an **Insert** command or icon (here it's the paper clip). This brings up the **Insert Attachment** box from which you choose the files you wish to send.

Some organizations are wary of receiving attachments from unknown sources because they could carry a virus. Check how companies feel about attachments before sending them and that they have compatible software to read your files. If, for example, you send a Word 97 document to someone who has Word 6, the formatting will be lost and replaced by gobbledy-gook.

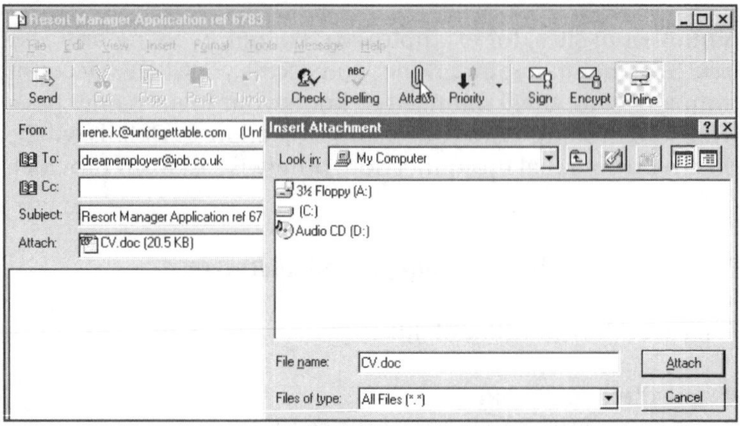

Figure A1.14 Any file on your computer can be sent as an e-mail attachment

NEWSGROUPS

Newsgroups are 'places' where people with similar interests exchange views, ask questions, offer help, bicker and occasionally insult one another. Contributors can be experts in their field or weird eccentrics. You should take the same precautions as you would in other parts of the internet.

Understanding newsgroup names

With over 40,000 newsgroups you need to know how to select the right ones. Each has a unique name made up of several parts and these give you an indication of the subjects they deal with. The first part of the name tells you which category it comes into. Common ones are:

alt.	Alternative newsgroups. Very much informal and unofficial sources of information.
biz.	Cover commercial and business matters.
comp.	Computer related discussion. A good place for tips from experts.
misc.	A catch-all for subjects that don't fit anywhere else.
uk.	Discussions with a British focus.
euro.	Discussions with a European focus.

The second part of the name gives you an indication of the specific subject they're dealing with. For example:

- uk.jobs.contract
- alt.building.jobs
- bermuda.jobs.offered
- bionet.jobs
- euro.jobs
- uk.jobs.fortyplus

Selecting and subscribing to newsgroups

Subscription is free and fully explained in the help section of the software that comes with mail software and is similar to it. Initially you need to go online to receive the full list of newsgroups kept by your ISP, which takes a few minutes, but then you can look at it offline. There is usually a facility to search for keywords so you don't have to go through the lot. Messages can be composed and read offline (see Figure A1.15).

Once you subscribe, new articles will be posted to you. They can be collected each time you go online in the same way as you collect mail. There may be hundreds of new articles each day for any one newsgroup, so avoid the temptation to subscribe to lots. You can choose to download message headers only, to save time, and then get the full text of anything interesting later. Posting to a newsgroup is like sending an e-mail. There's usually the option to reply to the author of a message or to the whole newsgroup.

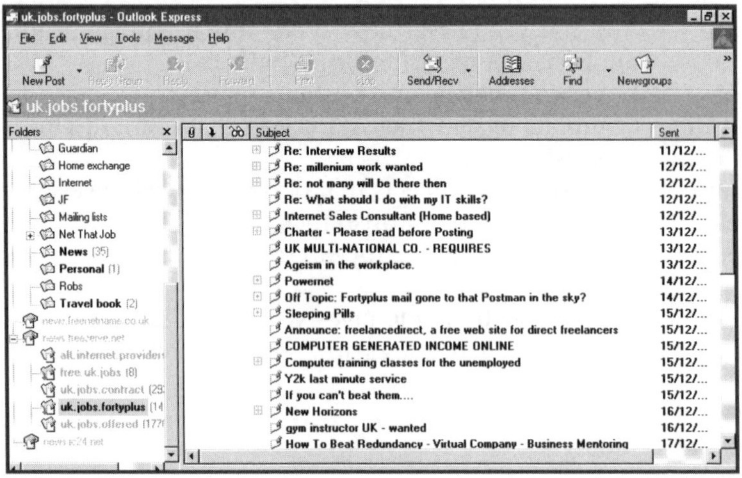

Figure A1.15 Join a discussion group that meets your interests

The many newsgroups related to job search and careers guidance can be useful resources, providing networking contacts, information on industry trends, access to vacancies and a place to post your CV, but they are even more unregulated than the Web. Career Mosaic offers links to job-related newsgroups and this is a good starting point (see Figure 4.10).

CHAT

This is a live discussion in which you can participate. Many recruitment sites offer the chance to 'talk' to other people about career related matters.

TIPS FOR COST-EFFECTIVE INTERNET USE

Investigate free calls and discount schemes.

The number of free providers continues to grow with many offering free calls as well. Check system requirements and hidden costs. Go for providers with POP 3 mail rather than a Web-based system. If you pay for internet calls, check whether your phone company offers discounts on frequently called numbers and add your ISP's internet access number.

Use the internet when it's cheap and fast.

Access the Web during cheap rate periods for phone calls and connect at times that are not busy. This varies depending where you live. At busy times you may fail to make connections and data transfer will be slower.

Access sites through Favorites.

Create **Favorites** offline so that time online is not spent typing in long URLs. Have the ones you want to visit at the top of your **Favorites** file.

Avoid slow-loading home pages.

A site's home page is not always the best one to select as your future starting point. Many take a long time to load. Subsequent pages are usually plainer and give access to the rest of the site.

Set your home page as a blank.

It means your computer won't try to dial up every time you open your browser. The home page of your ISP can be slow to load and may not be the place you always want to start from.

Stop images, sound and video clips being loaded automatically.

Set your browser not to include these and pages will take less time to load.

Don't try to read information on screen.

Go quickly to links that interest you, your eye will be drawn to them because they are coloured and have underlined text or pictures. Watch the status bar that tells you what's happening with your connections and data transfer. Once it says 'Done', or words to that effect, it has cached the link you requested and you can go back to where you started using the **Back** button. Read and print pages offline using **History**.

Compose all your e-mail messages offline and send several at a time.

Most e-mail software lets you store messages in an outbox. No matter how many messages and how diverse their destinations, they will all be sent as part of the same phone call. Use the address book facility to store frequently-used addresses.

Copy and paste e-mail for Web-based accounts.

If you are using a Web-based e-mail account and cannot compose offline, write your message using a word processing package and copy it to the clipboard. Then go online, access your e-mail site and paste the message in.

Plan ahead.

Have a clear idea of what you hope to get from a session on the internet before you connect. Have e-mails ready to send and sites to visit in **Favorites**. If you know that you're likely to get carried away, set a timer to jolt you out of your absorption.

Keep an eye on downloads.

When downloading software check the size of the files and the time transfer is likely to take. Don't go away and leave a long download, keep checking data is coming through and the clock is counting down. If something goes wrong, the data transfer can stop, but you are still paying for the telephone connection.

Only use the internet when it's appropriate.

Don't assume that the internet is the best way to research everything.

Give up when you're losing.

Both telephones and computers are wonderful tools when they work properly, and sources of immense frustration when they don't. There will inevitably be times when things go wrong. If things aren't working properly, it's a good idea to take a break. It may be fixed by the time you come back.

SITES WORTH SEEING

Internet courses and public access

Learn Direct England and Wales
www.learndirect.co.uk

Learn Direct Scotland
www.learning-direct-scotland.org.uk

Earl
www.earl.org.uk/access/indexloc.html
Details of libraries in the UK with public internet access.

Net Café Guide
www.netcafeguide.com
Comprehensive listing of cybercafés.

Internet Service Providers

Net 4 Nowt
www.net4nowt.com
The easiest way of keeping up to date with the best ISP offers as they happen. This site provides a really valuable service for all Web users who want to keep costs down.

Reliable free access providers include:

- Freeserve www.freeserve.net
- Tesco www.tesco.net
- IC24 www.ic24.net
- The BBC www.freebeeb.net
- Line One www.lineone.net
- Supanet www.supanet.com

Keeping safe

Consumer Gateway

www.consumer.gov.uk

This Department of Trade and Industry site has excellent information and advice for consumers. It explains your rights and links to Web sites with further advice and information.

Internet Watch Foundation

www.iwf.org.uk

Encourages internet users to report material that appears illegal.

NCH Action For Children: A Parents' Guide to the Internet

www.nchafc.org.uk/Internet/guide.html

'Children need to learn to be Net-Smart, then they can either avoid potentially risky people or situations, or know what to do if they come across them by accident. To be Net-Smart is an essential skill for the future. The truth is we all need to be Net-Smart, not just our children.'

Figure A1.16 Download a detailed internet safety guide from this site

Net Parents

www.netparents.org
US site providing resources for parents concerned about inappropriate material online. Lots of useful content and links.

Safe surf

www.safesurf.com
An organization working at making the internet safe for children without censorship. They have developed the SafeSurf Rating System, which you can add to Microsoft's **Content Explorer**.

Search tools

Multi-searchers include:

- www.dogpile.com
- www.savvysearch.com

UK specific searchers include:

- www.ukmax.co.uk
- www.ukdirectory.co.uk
- www.ukplus.co.uk
- www.yahoo.co.uk
- www.altavista.co.uk

Other search tools to try:

- www.google.com
- www.alltheWeb.com
- www.ask.com

For a comprehensive overview and update on search tools, look at www.searchenginewatch.com

Accessibility

BETSIE

www.bbc.co.uk/education/betsie
BBC Education's Text to Speech Internet Enhancer, see page 153.

Bobby
www.cast.org/bobby
Web-based service that analyses the accessibility of Web pages for people with disabilities.

Microsoft Accessibility and Disabilities Site
microsoft.com/enable
Information and utilities to download that customize earlier versions of Windows.

Trace Research and Development Centre
www.trace.wisc.edu
Publishes a database of computer products and provides related information for people with disabilities.

The Web Accessibility Initiative (WAI)
www.w3.org/WAI/References
Works at ensuring that internet technology is accessible to all and provides help for users and designers.

E-mail and newsgroups

E-mail addresses
www.emailaddresses.com

Figure A1.17 Find information on and links to every type of e-mail account

Email Booth: www.emailbooth.com
Twigger: www.twigger.co.uk
IC Messaging: www.icmessaging.co.uk
Examples of sites that let you pick up POP 3 mail from any computer.

Genie internet

www.genie.co.uk
Service from BT Cellnet that integrates internet and mobile phone use. The facility to send messages to any mobile phone from their site or one of their free email accounts is available to everyone, regardless of network or ISP used.

People Search

www.peoplesearch.net
Multi-search engine for e-mail addresses.

APPENDIX 2 – USEFUL SITES AT A GLANCE

CONTENTS

GENERAL INFORMATION

BBC Job Jungle
www.bbc.co.uk/education/workskills/jobs/index.shtml

BBC's Web Guide
www.bbc.co.uk/education/Webguide

The Biz
www.thebiz.co.uk

Careersoft
www.careersoft.co.uk

Citizens First
www.citizens.eu.int

Company Annual Reports on Line
www.carol.co.uk

Eurograduate
www.eurograduate.com

GTI Careerscape
www.gti.co.uk

Gradunet's Virtual Careers Office
www.gradunet.co.uk

Hoover's Corporate Web Sites
www.hoovers.com

Connexions Card
www.dfee.gov.uk/lcard

Learning Exchange
www.learningexchange.org.uk

National Training Organisations
www.nto-nc.org

Netwise
www.netwise.ac.uk

Plan-It
www.ceg.org.uk

Professional body links
www.niss.ac.uk/world/prof-bodies.html

Prospects Web
www.prospects.csu.ac.uk

SPECIFIC INFORMATION

Animals, plants and the environment

Animal Care and Equine Training Association
www.horsecareers.co.uk

British Horse Society
www.bhs.org.uk

British Trust for Conservation Volunteers
www.btcv.org.uk

British Veterinary Nursing Association
www.bvna.org.uk

Groundwork Trust
www.groundwork.org.uk

LANTRA
www.eto.co.uk

Nature Net
www.naturenet.net

Royal Horticultural Society
www.rhs.org.uk

Institute of Horticulture
www.horticulture.demon.co.uk

Royal College of Veterinary Surgeons
www.rcvs.org.uk

The Wildlife Trust
www.wildlifetrust.org.uk

Administration, business, clerical and management

Association of MBAs
www.mba.org.uk

British Computer Society
www.bcs.org.uk

Chartered Institute of Environmental Health
www.cieh.org.uk

Ergonomics Society
www.ergonomics.org.uk

Institute of Chartered Accountants of Scotland
www.icas.org.uk

Institute for the Management of Information Systems
www.imis.org.uk

Institute of Management
www.inst-mgt.org.uk

Institute of Personnel and Development
www.ipd.co.uk

Management Consultancies Association
www.mca.org.uk/html/careers.html

Operational Research Society
www.orsoc.org.uk

Armed forces, security and protective services

The Army
www.army.mod.uk

Fire Net
www.fire.org.uk

Maritime and Coastguard Agency
www.mcagency.org.uk

MI5
www.mi5.gov.uk

The Navy
www.royal-navy.mod.uk

Police UK
www.police.uk

Prison Service
www.hmprisonservice.gov.uk

The RAF
www.raf.mod.uk

Artistic and design-related work

Arts Council of England
www.artscouncil.org.uk

Association of Illustrators
www.aoi.co.uk

British Artists Blacksmiths Association
www.baba.org.uk

British Institute of Professional Photography
www.bipp.com/working.html

British Printing Industries Federation
www.bpif.org.uk

CAPITB Trust
www.careers-in-clothing.co.uk

Furniture Research Institute
www.furniture-unit.co.uk

The Society of British Theatre Designers (SBTD)
www.theatredesign.org.uk/train.htm

Buying, selling and related services

Advertising Association
www.adassoc.org.uk

Association of Exhibition Organisers
www.aeo.org.uk/careers/careers.html

Institute of Public Relations
www.ipr.org.uk

Chartered Institute of Purchasing and Supply
www.cips.org

Communications and Marketing Education Foundation
www.camfoundation.com

Market Research Society
www.marketresearch.org.uk

Construction and land services

British Cartographic Society
www.cartography.org.uk

British Institute of Architectural Technologists
www.biat.org.uk

British Plumbing Employers Council
www.bpec.org.uk

Construction Industry Training Board
www.citb.org.uk

Institute of Civil Engineers
www.ice.org.uk

Landscape Institute
www.l-i.org.uk and
www.1stlandscape.co.uk

Royal Institute of British Architects
www.architecture.com

Royal Institution of Chartered Surveyors
www.rics.org.uk

Royal Town Planning Institute
www.rtpi.org.uk

Engineering

British Horological Institute
www.bhi.co.uk

NET (NTO for the electrotechnical industry)
www.net-works.org.uk/careers.htm

Engineering Construction Training Board
www.ecitb.org.uk

Engineering Council
www.engc.org.uk

Engineering Marine Training Authority
www.emta.org.uk

Motor Industry Training Council
www.motor-careers.co.uk

Institute of Electrical Engineers
www.iee.org.uk

Institute of Marine Engineers
www.imare.org.uk

Institute of Materials
www.materials.org.uk

Institute of Petroleum
www.petroleum.co.uk

National Training Organisation for Oil and Gas Extraction
www.opito.co.uk

Royal Aeronautical Society
www.aerosociety.com

The Royal Institution of Naval Architects
www.rina.org.uk

Entertainment, leisure, sport and travel

Association of British Theatre Technicians
www.abtt.org.uk

Ballet
www.ballet.co.uk

British Film Institute
www.bfi.org.uk

British Phonographic Industry Limited
www.bpi.co.uk

Classical Music UK
www.classicalmusic.co.uk

Council for Dance
www.cdet.org.uk

Eejit's guide to Film-Making
www.exposure.co.uk/eejit/index.html

Equity
www.equity.org.uk

Incorporated Society of Musicians
www.ism.org

Institute of Leisure and Amenity Management
www.ilam.co.uk

Institute Of Sport and Recreation Management (ISRM)
www.isrm.co.uk

Metier
www.metier.org.uk

Models UK
www.models.co.uk

The Moving Image Society
www.bksts.com

Mandy's International Film and TV Production Directory
www.mandy.com

National Coaching Foundation
www.ncf.org.uk

National Council for Drama Training
www.ncdt.co.uk

PGL Adventure Holidays
www.pgl.co.uk

Skillset
www.skillset.org

Travel Training Company
www.tttc.co.uk

Finance and related work

Association of Accounting Technicians
www.aat.co.uk

Association of Chartered Certified Accountants
www.acca.co.uk

Chartered Institute of Management Accountants
www.cima.org.uk

Chartered Institute of Public Finance Accountancy
www.cipfa.org.uk

Chartered Insurance Institute
www.cii.co.uk

Faculty and Institute of Actuaries
www.actuaries.org.uk

Institute of Chartered Accountants in England & Wales (ICAEW)
www.icaew.co.uk

LIFFEnet Trader Centre
www.liffe.com

Securities Institute
www.securities-institute.org.uk

Health and medical services

Association of the British Pharmaceutical Industry
www.abpi.org.uk

Association of Theatre Personnel Nationwide
www.tpn.org.uk

Anglo European College of Chiropractic
www.aecc.ac.uk

Association for Medical Education
www.asme.org.uk

British College of Naturopathy & Osteopathy
www.bcno.org.uk

British Dental Association
www.bda-dentistry.org.uk

British Dietetic Association
www.bda.uk.com

British Medical Journal
www.bmj.com

Chartered Society of Physiotherapy
www.csp.org.uk

College of Occupational Therapists
www.cot.co.uk
www.baot.co.uk

Institute of Complementary Medicine
www.icmedicine.co.uk

English Nursing Board
www.enb.org.uk

General Osteopathic Council
www.osteopathy.org.uk

Horticulture Therapy
www.thrive.org.uk

Nurses and Midwives Admissions Service
www.nmas.ac.uk

NHS
www.nhs50.nhs.uk

Nursing Board for Scotland
www.nbs.org.uk

Nursing Board for Wales
www.wnb.org.uk

Reflexology
www.reflexology.org

Royal College of Speech and Language Therapists
www.rcslt.org

Society of Chiropodists and Podiatrists
www.feetforlife.org/career.htm

Hospitality, catering and other services

Barzone
www.barzone.co.uk

Brewers and Licensed Retailers Association
www.blra.co.uk

Cleaning and Support Services National Training Organisation
www.cleaningnto.org

Hairdressing and Beauty Industry Authority
www.habia.org.uk

Hospitality Training Foundation
www.htf.org.uk

Hotel and Catering International Management Association
www.hcima.org.uk

Hotel and Catering Training Company
www.hctc.co.uk

Springboard
www.springboarduk.org.uk

Law and related work

Chartered Institute of Patent Agents
www.cipa.org.uk

General Council of the Bar
www.barcouncil.org.uk

Institute of Legal Executives
www.ilex.org.uk

Institute of Trade Mark Attorneys
www.itma.org.uk

Law Careers Net
www.lawcareers.net

Law Society
www.lawsociety.org.uk

Scottish Law Society
www.lawscot.org.uk

Student Law Centre
www.studentlaw.com

Sciences, mathematics and related work

Association of British Science Writers
www.absw.org.uk

British Geological Survey
www.bgs.ac.uk

British National Space Centre
www.highview.co.uk

Gem Association of Great Britain
www.gagtl.ac.uk

Geological Society
www.geolsoc.org.uk

Institute of Food Science & Technology
www.ifst.org

Institute of Biology
www.iob.org

Institute of Biomedical Science
www.ibms.org

Institute of Physics
www.iop.org

Royal Astronomical Society
www.ras.org.uk

Royal Society of Chemistry
www.chemistry.rsc.org

Society for Underwater Technology
www.sut.org.uk

Social and related services

Association of Educational Psychologists
www.aep.org.uk

British Association of Counselling
www.bac.co.uk

British Psychological Society
www.bps.org.uk

Council for Education and Training in Social Work (CCETSW)
www.ccetsw.org.uk

National Childminders Association
www.ncma.org.uk

Appendix 2

Teaching and cultural activities

Broadcast Journalism Training Council
www.bjtc.org.uk

Church Mission Society
www.cms-uk.org

Council for British Archaeology
www.britarch.ac.uk

Cultural Heritage National Training Organisation
www.chnto.co.uk

General Teaching Council for Scotland
www.gtcs.org.uk

Institute of Linguists
www.iol.org.uk

Institute of Translation and Interpreting
www.iti.org.uk

Languages NTO
www.languagesnto.org.uk

Library Association
www.la-hq.org.uk

National Council for the Training of Journalists
www.nctj.com

National Youth Agency
www.nya.org.uk

Periodical Publishers Association
www.ppa.co.uk

Publishers Association
www.publishers.org.uk

Society of Archivists
www.archives.org.uk

Society of Indexers
www.socind.demon.co.uk

Teacher Training Agency
www.teach-tta.gov.uk

Training Zone
www.trainingzone.co.uk

Writers' Guild of Great Britain
www.writers.org.uk

Transport

British Air Line Pilots Association
www.balpa.org.uk

Chamber of Shipping
www.british-shipping.org

Institute of Logistics and Transport
www.iolt.org.uk

Marine Society
www.marine-society.org

National Air Traffic Services
www.nats.co.uk

Rail careers
www.ritc.org.uk

Road Haulage and Distribution Training Council
www.rhdtc.co.uk

Transfed
www.transfed.org.uk

ALTERNATIVE WORK STYLES

European Telework Online
www.eto.org.uk

The UK Teleworkers
www.tca.org.uk

Flexibility
www.flexibility.co.uk

Freelance Centre
www.freelancecentre.com

Smarter Work
www.smarterwork.com

Working From Home
www.workingfromhome.co.uk

DISABILITY ISSUES

CanDo: Disability Careers Network
www.cando.lancs.ac.uk

Employability
www.nrec.org.uk/employability

RNIB
www.rnib.org.uk

Skill
www.skill.org.uk

Workable
www.members.aol.com/workableuk

EMPLOYERS

Air 2000
www.air2000.ltd.uk

Andersen Consulting
www.careers.ac.com

Arcadia Group
www.principles.co.uk

Asda
www.asda.co.uk

BBC
www.bbc.co.uk

British Airways
www.british-airways.com/inside/employme/employme.shtml

European Commission
www.cec.org.uk

Government Communications Headquarters (GCHQ)
www.gchq.gov.uk

Hewlett Packard:
www.jobs.hp.com

KPMG
www.kpmgcareers.co.uk

MI5
www.mi5.gov.uk

Microsoft
www.microsoft.com/uk/jobs

Police Services UK
www.police.uk

PriceWaterhouseCoopers
www.pwcglobal.com

Shell International
www.shell.com

SmithKlineBeecham
www.sb.com

Thomson's Holidays
www.thomson-holidays.com

Unilever
www.uniq.unilever.com

VOLUNTARY AND NOT FOR PROFIT

BOND: British Overseas NGOs for Development
www.bond.org.uk

Community Service Volunteers
www.csv.org.uk

National Centre for Volunteering
www.volunteering.org.uk

Voluntary Service Overseas
www.vso.org.uk

World Service Enquiry
www.wse.org.uk

SELF-ASSESSMENT AND TEST SITES

BBC Education
www.bbc.co.uk/education/workskills/wow/match.shtml

Birkman Quiz
www.review.com/birkman

CareerStorm
www.careerstorm.com

Civil Service Fast Stream Assessment Package
www.selfassess.faststream.gov.uk

INTEC
www.intec.edu.za/career/career.htm

Keirsey Temperament Sorter
www.keirsey.com

Morrisby Organisation
www.morrisby.co.uk

Queeendom
www.queendom.com

SHL
www.shldirect.com

Standard Life
www.lifeoutlined.co.uk

The Big Trip
www.thebigtrip.co.uk

Two H
www.2h.com

University of Waterloo, Canada
www.careerservices.uwaterloo.ca/manual-home.html

Wide Eyes
www.wideeyes.com

Appendix 2

VACANCY SOURCES

Newspapers

E&P Directory of Online Newspapers
www.emedia1.mediainfo.com/emedia

Kidon Media-Link
www.kidon.com/media-link

Financial Times
www.ft.com

Fish 4 Jobs
www.fish4jobs.co.uk

The Guardian (vacancies)
www.jobsunlimited.co.uk

Rise
www.jobsunlimited.co.uk/rise

Irish Times
www.ireland.com

The Telegraph (vacancies)
www.appointments-plus.com

The Times (vacancies)
www.revolver.com

Times Educational Supplement (vacancies)
www.jobs.tes.co.uk

The Times Higher Education Supplement (vacancies)
www.jobs.thes.co.uk

Professional and trade journals

British Medical Journal
www.bmj.com

The Caterer and Hotelkeeper
www.caterer.com

Computer Weekly
www.computerweekly.co.uk

Careers in Construction
www.careersinconstruction.com

Dalton's Weekly
www.daltons.co.uk

Estates Gazette
www.egi.co.uk

Flight International
www.flightinternational.com

Health Service Journal
www.hsj.co.uk

Housing Today
www.housingtoday.org.uk

In Brief
www.inbrief.co.uk

LGC Net
www.lgcnet.com

Marketing Online
www.marketing.haynet.com

Nature
www.nature.com

New Scientist
www.newscientist.com

Physics World Jobs
physicsweb.org/jobs

Therapy Weekly
www.therapy.co.uk

The Stage
www.thestage.co.uk

Employment agencies

Academic Jobs
www.jobs.ac.uk

Active Connection
www.activeconnection.co.uk

Aupair JobMatch
www.aupairs.co.uk

Capital Markets Consulting Ltd
www.cmcx.com

Capita RAS
www.rasnet.co.uk

Career Mosaic
www.careermosaic-uk.co.uk

Charity People
www.charitypeople.co.uk

Cool Works
www.coolworks.com

Digitext
www.digitext.co.uk

EURES – European Employment Service
www.europa.eu.int/jobs/eures

FÁS – Training & Employment Authority (Ireland)
www.fas.ie

FoodJobs
www.foodjobs.co.uk

Gis-a-Job
www.gisajob.com

International Guild of Professional Butlers and Private Personnel Ltd
www.butlersguild.com

Job Site
www.jobsite.co.uk

The Monster Board
www.monster.co.uk

People Bank
www.peoplebank.com

Price Jamieson
www.pricejam.co.uk

Public Sector Recruitment
www.psr-agency.com

Recruitment & Employment Confederation
www.rec.uk.com

Reed
www.reed.co.uk

Stepstone
www.stepstone.co.uk

Taps
www.taps.com

TEFL Professional Network
www.tefl.com

Thomas Telford Recruitment
www.t-telford.co.uk

Top Jobs
www.topjobs.co.uk

Total Jobs
www.totaljobs.com

Wideyes
www.wideyes.com

Young Scientist
www.young-scientist.co.uk

UK Employment Service
www.employmentservice.gov.uk

GLOSSARY

attachment Any text, picture, sound or video file sent with an e-mail.

bit Short for 'binary digit', it is the smallest unit of information stored on a computer. The speed at which a modem transfers data is measured in bits per second (bps).

bookmark A stored internet address file which gives access to that site with a single click of the mouse. Other names for this include hotlist and favorite.

broadband High speed internet access.

browser Software that enables you to view documents on the World Wide Web.

cache The cache stores the information downloaded from the internet on your computer. This enables you to reload quickly on subsequent visits and to look at pages offline.

chat Live conversation by typing in messages.

cookie Small file sent to and stored on your computer. It enables the host site to recognize you and remember personal preferences and settings.

cybercafe A cafe with computers where you can eat, drink and access the internet. A growing phenomenon.

download Transfer of information from a computer on the internet to your own computer.

e-mail Short for electronic mail. A system for sending messages and files from one internet linked computer to another.

encryption Writing messages in coded form to ensure they can only be read by recipients who have the key to that code.

FAQ Frequently Asked Question. Web sites and newsgroups have lists of these to help you make good use of what they offer (and to prevent you being a nuisance by asking something that's already been asked thousands of times).

file Anything stored on your computer – documents, pictures, videos and programs.
freeware Software that is completely free.
FTP File Transfer Protocol. A method of transferring files from one computer to another.
gateway sites These act as signposts; they contain links to large numbers of other sites on a particular topic.
hard disc The part of your computer where information is stored. Floppy discs are a smaller version of this and can be used to move files between computers.
HTML Hyper Text Markup Language. The computer language in which Web pages are written. You don't need to understand it unless you want to write Web pages of your own. To see what it looks like, go to View/Source for any Web page.
hypertext link An image or piece of text on a Web page that provides a link to another site or document.
Intranet A mini-internet within an organization. Most universities and schools have an intranet on their network of computers. This can be kept private or made accessible to general Web users.
Internet A worldwide network of linked computers.
Internet Service Provider (ISP) The organization that provides you with internet access.
modem The device that connects your computer to the phone network.
netiquette Internet etiquette. A loose set of 'rules' about how to behave when using the internet that particularly applies to newsgroups.
newsgroup An internet discussion group. There are groups for every topic imaginable.
offline browser Software that allows you to view previously accessed Web pages and links without connecting to the internet.
online Connected to the internet via the phone network.
plug-ins Software that allows your computer to perform extra functions, sometimes necessary to view a Web page properly. Most pages that require a plug-in offer links to free downloads.
Point of Presence (POP) The phone number that connects you to your ISP.
search engine/directory A facility that acts as an index to the internet and allows you to search for relevant documents.

shareware Software that can be tried out for free for a limited period. Continued use requires a fee to be paid to the author.

SSL (Secure Sockets Layer) Internet security system that encodes the data you send so no one can read or change them during transmission. Financial transactions and transfer of other sensitive data should be done only through secure sites.

Uniform Resource Locator (URL) The address of a Web site. Every Web page has a unique URL.

virus A virus is designed to disrupt the working of a computer. They can be transferred from one computer to another. It is essential to install software that checks for viruses before you download anything from the Web. If you have a virus it can also be 'cleaned up' by this software.

Web page A document viewed on the Web. It can be several paper pages long.

Web site A collection of Web pages.

World Wide Web The most widely used part of the internet. It allows publication of and access to documents. Also referred to as WWW, W3 and the Web.

INDEX

Web sites in this index are in the main sections of the book; additional sites can be found in Appendix 2 and are not indexed here

INDEX OF ADVERTISERS